SpringerBriefs in Health Care Management and Economics

Series editor
Joseph K. Tan, McMaster University, Burlington, ON, Canada

More information about this series at http://www.springer.com/series/10293

James S. Powers

Creating a Value Proposition for Geriatric Care

The Transformation of American Healthcare

 Springer

James S. Powers
Department of Medicine
Vanderbilt University Medical Center
Nashville, Tennessee, USA

ISSN 2193-1704   ISSN 2193-1712 (electronic)
SpringerBriefs in Health Care Management and Economics
ISBN 978-3-319-62270-5   ISBN 978-3-319-62271-2   (eBook)
DOI 10.1007/978-3-319-62271-2

Library of Congress Control Number: 2017945754

Printed on acid-free paper

This Springer imprint is published by Springer Nature
The registered company is Springer International Publishing AG
The registered company address is: Gewerbestrasse 11, 6330 Cham, Switzerland

Contents

Contents

About the Author

James S. Powers is Professor of Medicine at Vanderbilt University School of Medicine and Associate Clinical Director at the Tennessee Valley Healthcare System, Geriatric Research Education and Clinical Center (TVHS GRECC), Nashville, TN. He is the Geriatrics Fellowship Program Director. The views expressed are his own and based on his experience of over three decades as a primary care and geriatrics care model innovator with experience consulting, developing, evaluating, and sustaining healthcare models and health professions educational programs throughout the Mid-South. He has remained at the same institutions long enough to see culture change, and programs take hold, remain sustained, and grow. He shares with the reader the continuing gaps, barriers, and challenges to advancing and promoting geriatric programs, as well as addressing the critical topics of sustainment and succession planning. It is the author's hope that the development of academic and clinical programs, the creative strategies applied, and the outcomes and lessons learned will be applicable to the development of other healthcare models. Dr. Powers focuses on quality improvement and evaluating educational and clinical outcomes, maintains a large clinical practice, and teaches geriatrics to healthcare professionals of all disciplines.

Chapter 1
Introduction

Abstract Change is difficult and slow. The role of the agent of change is no less so. This book is about the long journey involved in achieving healthcare changes. Health care is complicated. Included are many practical principles, tools, and examples to guide other change agents to help them achieve their vision, aggregate the required collaboration and support, and overcome barriers-all of which are the nature of change. It is the author's firm belief that care for older adults and the development of Geriatrics as a discipline provides many compelling models of care with far-reaching influences contributing to the transformation of American Health Care.

This book is about change and the role of the agent of change. It was conceived during a career–long effort to promote geriatric care for an aging society, and as an introspective guide for other change agents as they champion their own causes. It is not written for those born with silver spoons in their mouths – those destined for rapid rise to power, influence, and blessed with the ability to easily convince others, gain support, and establish their programs -if indeed there are any individuals out there in this category. They do not need this book, and we can all learn from you! It is for those who struggle over years and throughout their careers to achieve a vision and overcome the many barriers inherent in change. This book is for you.

United States is undergoing a value–based healthcare transformation.

This book is about creating a value proposition – a promise of value to be delivered to improve care to and to provide specific benefits to healthcare systems. Included are strategies and an understanding of the incentives and barriers encountered in promoting changes in the healthcare system. The perspective is that of a physician who has worked with administrators, colleagues, policy makers, educators, and patients and their families. Numerous examples and outcomes are discussed coming from a clinical and academic perspective and from having worked in the Veterans Administration. However the forces that these institutions have responded to, in addition to the aging imperative, will hopefully provide guidance for other healthcare systems as well. Is also the hope of the author that the information contained will help guide the introduction of geriatric principles into mainstream medical care with the goal of improving the care and quality of life for older persons in all healthcare systems.

© Springer International Publishing AG 2017   1
J.S. Powers, *Creating a Value Proposition for Geriatric Care*, SpringerBriefs in
Health Care Management and Economics, DOI 10.1007/978-3-319-62271-2_1

The development of geriatric programs to care for an aging America is not of recent origin. The term Geriatrics was coined in the 1880s, and the American Geriatrics Society was founded in 1942. Despite this, the field is still slowly developing. While other areas of medicine have witnessed tremendous advances during the twentieth century, such as the development of antibiotics for infectious diseases, new therapies for diabetes and cardiovascular disease, as well as treatments for cancers, Geriatrics has remained on the back burner in the view of many. Despite a burgeoning elderly population with projections of great needs for geriatric care, and pleading for more geriatric care by the public, there have been many barriers to developing geriatric care programs. The World Health Organization projects that there will be a doubling of individuals age 65 and older in developing countries, and an increase to over 20% of the population over age 65 in most developed countries [1]. We know that elderly patients expend the greatest amount of healthcare resources in the 6 months prior to death, and disproportionately utilize medications and healthcare services at two to three times the rate of the rest of the population [2]. Yet the US has focused on medical specialization and procedure-oriented care, resulting in a shortage of primary care, poor coordination of care and greatly increased costs. The United States ranks 37th in health outcomes despite the highest overall expenditure for healthcare [3].

Why then has it been so difficult to develop geriatric programs? Does Geriatrics have no voice? Do the elderly have no advocates? Surely population needs and expectations are not being met. Each year a disproportionate share of America medical school graduates choose non-primary care specialties and enter residencies paid for by the Medicare education allotment. Medical training institutions remain free to utilize these training funds to further the growth of specialty care, enhance local prestige, and to provide highly profitable services. Despite decades of building innovative geriatric educational programs and providing training opportunities in Geriatrics, trainees – the future medical providers, have not been coming. Rather they have been influenced by the specialty interests of their training institutions, fully supported by current CMS policies and training funding support. Political and economic forces have provided critical influences to shape medical education, career choices, the organization of the American healthcare system and its care delivery models.

There are other reasons that geriatric care has been overlooked as well. Frail older individuals are poor advocates for their own health. Person-centered care of older individuals is a primary care focus which is poorly reimbursed and requires constant, sustained, and difficult work on the part of the provider. Family caregivers realize the need for these services; however they often are in a poor position to provide a collective voice to counter powerful lobbying groups including teaching hospitals, specialty physicians, and healthcare corporations. We need to raise consumer awareness and encourage the public to voice their concerns. They have the collective power to demand change and drive policy. Additionally, more and more boomers are getting older, are well-educated and concerned, and may have much to add to the conversation.

Table 1.1 Developer-change agent skills

1.	Future oriented
2.	Persistence
3.	Ability to market, rebrand
4.	Remain helpful
5.	Seek overlapping benefits
6.	Arrange new alliances, reformulate teams
7.	Be grateful

Table 1.2 Developer-change agent tools

1.	Historical perspective
2.	Reflect from an external framework
3.	Process orientation
4.	Be helpful

This book is about the efforts of Geriatrics as a field to overcome the barriers inherent in establishing a new field and competing with special interests in order to establish appropriate standards of care, geriatric care models, administer effective education programs, and advance knowledge specific to the care of older adults. The principles discussed in the following chapters are drawn from many fields including Medicine, the Biological Sciences, Sociology, Politics, Business, and Economics. The examples provided and the generalizations that are drawn are varied and are meant to demonstrate the many strategies required to build programs, surmount barriers, obtain and demonstrate early successes, sustain efforts, and inspire future direction. It is the hope of the author that the examples will be of interest to colleagues world-wide as they labor to establish and sustain person-centric geriatric care models appropriate to their own settings. In creating geriatric care programs, they will inevitably be exposed to a number of barriers including corporations, political interests, government entities, and professional societies. They too will need to rely on supportive colleagues, an informed and interested public, knowledge of geriatric standards of care and best practices, and be armed with examples of successful and sustainable programs.

In my experience the successful change agent will require a number of skills (Table 1.1) and rely on a number of tools (Table 1.2). The agent of change must look into the future, have a vision and goal in mind and remain sustained over what may be a prolonged implementation process. The agent of change functions as a champion and will encounter numerous barriers erected by vested interests, but must persist in order to ultimately be successful. The cause will become your passion and calling. The ability to rebound, rebrand, find collaborators and develop coalitions to support progress is essential. Not every effort will be successful and the change agent must change strategies many times in order to be ultimately successful. A singularly important strategy involves remaining helpful to others as the change agent builds coalitions and shares the rewards of progress. Overlapping and mutually advantageous benefits are important incentives to identify and their creation an important strategy. It is important to reformulate teams and to invite willing participants. Being inclusive allows one to form new alliances and adopt fresh strategies. The agent of change must be eternally grateful for all assistance and to value rather than criticize help. Rewards should be shared gratefully with all participants as community ownership of any program is the key to sustainability.

The agent of change should be aware that tools are necessary in order to achieve success. An historical perspective is of enormous help in order to learn from others and to prevent repeated errors. Inviting the perspectives of others to help reframe strategies is essential. No one individual can see all perspectives and the wise agent of change benefits from the reflections of others. The change agent should realize that change is in reality a process, and being oriented to process facilitates strategy. There is a long process of pre-work or development of enabling factors necessary for success. Strategic timing is critical in implementing any change and change may progress through many strategic PDSA (plan-do-study-act) cycles in the process of achieving organizational change. PDSA cycles were originally conceived by Deming of Bell Labs as a process improvement tool, and they can be of great help to the change agent in refining strategy.

The agent of change will benefit from a long-term historical perspective and to avoid the mistakes that litter the pages of history. Viewing programmatic development from the perspective of the beholder is a virtue that cannot be underestimated, and physicians often demonstrate this skill, have a goal-oriented strategy and a process for obtaining results. And overall, be helpful in constructing programs that meet mutually beneficial objectives.

A note about the authentic examples used in this book. These have been chronicled from many sources throughout the author's consulting career. Some facts have been altered to preserve anonymity. As with true life experiences, changes occurred over differing amounts of time, some spanning decades. Sequels to three examples demonstrate strategic developmental sequences instructive in their own right, and are described in subsequent chapters with cross referencing provided. Within each example, the reader may advance to the sequel in order to immediately follow outcomes, or progress in a topical order through each chapter as desired. With these basic tenants, we proceed to discuss transformational healthcare changes exemplified by the development of geriatric programs in the United States.

References

1. An Aging World 2015. International population reports. https://www.census.gov/content/dam/Census/library/publications/2016/demo/p95-16-1.pdf. Accessed 3 Apr 2017.
2. National Health Expenditures (NHE) Fact Sheet. https://www.cms.gov/research-statistics-data-and-systems/statistics-trends-and-reports/nationalhealthexpenddata/nhe-fact-sheet.html. Accessed 3 Apr 2017.
3. The world health report 2000 – health systems: improving performance. Geneva: World Health Organization; 2000.

Chapter 2
US Geriatrics, an Historical Perspective

Abstract The greatest success of the twentieth century has been a doubling of life expectancy. The next challenge will be to increase the quality of life throughout that lifespan. Person-centered care and value-based models of care have always been part of Geriatrics from its very beginnings. Not only older adults, but their caregivers are demanding transparency and high-quality person-centered care. Changes in healthcare financing are inevitable, but an emphasis on value-based healthcare transformation is unlikely to change as total spending on healthcare approaches 20% of the GDP.

The greatest success of the twentieth century has been a doubling of life expectancy. The next challenge will be to increase the quality of life throughout that lifespan. We truly need a transformation of the healthcare system in order to accomplish this goal.

The development of Geriatrics in the United States is acknowledged with the start of the American Geriatrics Society in 1942. The Baltimore longitudinal study of aging was initiated in 1958. Shortly thereafter, the earliest beginnings of the American hospice movement began with Connecticut hospice, spearheaded by the Yale University School of Nursing in the mid – 1960s. The passage of the Older Americans Act, and Medicare in 1965 further highlighted care of older adults in the United States. The National Institute on Aging began in 1975. The Department of Veterans Affairs showed great interest in geriatrics due to the increasing age of WW2 Veterans which by the mid-1970s equaled three times the rate of aging in the general population. In 1975 the Geriatric Research Education and Clinical Centers (GRECC) program was developed and now includes 20 centers of excellence in the majority of the VA regions in the United States. These programs served to stimulate the growth of geriatrics and geriatrics training at affiliated university medical centers. The Omnibus Budget Reconciliation Act (OBRA) of 1987, passed as a result of congressional concern about conditions in nursing homes, established the requirement for a medical director in all US nursing homes, and has subsequently established numerous codes of federal regulations (CFR's) and quality improvement metrics to enhance quality and to improve transparency of care. Federal control of long term care is exercised through funding mechanisms rather than public health law. Facilities have conditions of participation (COP's) in order to participate in

© Springer International Publishing AG 2017   5
J.S. Powers, *Creating a Value Proposition for Geriatric Care*, SpringerBriefs in
Health Care Management and Economics, DOI 10.1007/978-3-319-62271-2_2

federal insurance programs. Nursing Home Compare was the first publicly reported quality report card, initiated in 2002. Many other consumer tools are also developing as value-based healthcare increases in prominence. The US is still the only country in the world that requires a medical director in all nursing homes.

Universities saw Geriatrics as a credible field of study and initiated geriatric programs in the 1970s at UCLA, and Johns Hopkins. Luminaries such as Robert Butler and David Solomon in the United States, following the lead of Marjorie Warren and John Brocklehurst from England, were early leaders advocating for patient-centric care of frail elderly, those afflicted with Alzheimer's disease, and for family and caregiver support services.

Our own experience in Tennessee mirrors that of most of the rest of the country. Program development was quietly begun without much fanfare by small interdisciplinary groups of interested individuals at university medical centers. Nursing Home Physicians formed a nonprofit Tennessee Association of Long Term Care Physicians in 1977. Geriatric nurse practitioner training started in 1985. The Tennessee Geriatric Society was started in 1986 by group of concerned Tennessee physicians as a local affiliate of the American Geriatric Society. The Federal Health Services Research Administration (HRSA) funded a Geriatric Education Center at East Tennessee State University (ETSU) in 1989 and at Meharry Medical College in 1990, focusing on interdisciplinary geriatric education for all healthcare professionals.

Administrations at US medical schools were largely unaware of the need for geriatric education and the activities of interested health professionals working in Geriatrics. Development of the field grew slowly, without any resistance, but without the benefit of administrative support. Program development succeeded by cooperation among regional educational programs through networking. Joint conferences and sharing of resources allowed collaboration among existing programs. The first certificate of added qualification (CAQ) for Geriatrics was offered by the American Board of Internal Medicine and the Academy of Family Practice in 1988.

Geriatrics is at heart a patient and family-centered specialty with a strong primary care focus which includes continuity of care, and caregiver support. Geriatrics represents a set of principles for complex decision making managing high cost, high need patients. The wisdom of geriatrics is that a person-centered approach produces care models to achieve both patient goals of care as well as cost–effective care. It is a linchpin for efforts to create successful value–based models of care.

General growth of the field is hampered by poor reimbursement and the general disdain of new medical graduates to enter primary care. The average primary care physician spends 1–3 h of documentation, paperwork, electronic medical record tasks, and patient follow-up for every 1 h of direct patient care [1]. This has got to change if we ever expect to increase the number of primary care and geriatric physicians! There are currently 6000 geriatricians in the United States, a number far below those required to care for frail elderly, let alone addressing prevention and primary care for older adults. Many geriatricians function as educators, consulting with and training other physicians to be good geriatricians for their own patients. Many others serve as interdisciplinary team leaders in acute and post-acute care settings, hospice and palliative care services; managing transitions of care for complex care patients, as well as high need older adults defined as those with dementia and deficits in activities of daily living. The Medicare Current Beneficiary Survey (MCBS) estimates that there are over five million community dwelling elderly individuals currently suffering from serious impairments [2].

Despite the great demand for geriatric services in the population, the prevailing concept is that the need for services and care for older adults is an individual family-related concern. Due to caregiving responsibilities, caregivers themselves are in a poor position to publicly advocate for services for themselves or their families. There is still little collective voice or public support promoting or demanding geriatric program development. While there are required courses for medical trainees in geriatrics, there is still little exposure to continuity of care, post-acute and long-term care, and caregiver concerns which are at the heart of the public demand for geriatric care. There is an educational–clinical care mismatch, as well as a disconnect between public expectations and the promotion of geriatric training programs.

Caregiver support also falls far below the public expectations. Caregivers for high need older adults often endure a 20 year-long career and they must navigate a complex healthcare system, long-term care support and services network (LTSS). Employers tell us that sandwich generation employees, those with younger dependents as well as aging parents, take far more time off to care for older and infirm family members than younger employees who occasionally stay home with a sick child. This should come as no surprise as the US Census Bureau estimates that the number of individuals greater than age 65 will exceed the number of school age children by 2020 [3]. We also know that caregivers' own health suffers and that they need support services and respite to accomplish their very difficult and emotion-laden tasks. The Alzheimer's Association reports the numbers of individuals living with Alzheimer's disease is expected to be 14 million by 2050 [4], coinciding with an increase age of the population. Some 90% of Alzheimer's care involves addressing caregiver concerns. It is critical to raise consumer awareness, and to reframe issues to move policy to support geriatric care issues [5].

There is a pervasive public misunderstanding regarding Aging that creates barriers to the development of the field of Geriatrics. We need frame the conversation about social services to move attitudes, knowledge, and preferences. We need to build an understanding and generate support for public policy solutions. If the public thinks of old age as one of decline and deterioration, it is no wonder that the cultural model suggests the general public does not want to be part of this identification. However, it is critical to shift the conversation to engage a collective action targeted to make a difference to improve the quality of life of older persons.. We need an innovative approach to create values and a social climate conducive to the needs of older adults. To do this we need to make a change and tell an alternative story to change the framework to one of hopeful expectations, maximizing quality of life, and instilling the realization that we are all in this together – all of us in reality are aging and currently living on one point of the time line.

The Aging Community is actively engaged in determining the best way to brand their services and the field of Geriatrics in order to engage the public. Most of the public consider aging an individual problem which affects others. Some 80% of individuals in the work force have no idea how they will cover long-term care service needs, and Medicare expends twice the amount for those with functional impairment when added to disease processes.

We desperately need a huge public awareness campaign to shift the public discourse to encourage collective responsibility. We must also train healthcare service providers to recognize, engage and support caregivers. This effort may be aided by a healthcare transformation to value- based purchasing which may help to motivate providers to engage caregivers more effectively.

The Frameworks Institute, in collaboration with the Aging Community, is engaged in a multi-year effort to change the conversation about aging by preparing and marketing the message: Aging is not an individual but a societal concern. The goal of this inventive campaign is to build a momentum, creating a public understanding of well-being for all individuals across the age continuum [6]. If the public gets this message and individuals see themselves as part of the aging continuum rather than spared, if we can change the conversation from them to us and emphasize that we are the agents of change, then we'll all reap the collective benefits of this paradigm shift.

The US needs to catch up with the healthcare solutions Geriatrics has developed. Geriatricians have a vast knowledge about caring for older persons. They understand risk stratification and targeting of intensive care-management, critical to achieving improved outcomes and savings. They understand and know how to address service delivery barriers to integrating medical services. They also have demonstrated an extraordinary and sustained commitment to improving the quality of life for older people. This value-added input is not clearly recognized by physician peers or healthcare organizations and Geriatrics needs to be mainstreamed to be effective [7, 8].

Geriatric models of care include many approaches to care that are proven to be more effective in treating older people when appropriately targeted and applied. These include access, design, and outcome assessments in primary care settings, disease state management programs, hospital and post-acute care settings. Systems struggle to move from fee for service and volume-based care to value-based care. Geriatric principles are more and more important for managing high cost, complex patients and the care of individuals with multiple chronic conditions. Geriatricians can provide leadership for health systems interventions in order to optimize care transitions and care coordination. These models demonstrate maintenance of function, cost avoidance, and reduced complications for selected frail elderly populations. They provide solutions benefitting older adults in proven and cost-effective ways that enhance quality throughout the healthcare system.

Geriatrics healthcare professionals also have special talents. They strive to optimize quality of life and independence. They use an interdisciplinary team approach. They integrate medical and social care. They provide services in multiple settings. These talents are especially important in determining goals of care normal aging versus disease, the care of individuals with geriatric syndromes as opposed to organ and disease based concerns. These skills are critical for the care of individuals with multiple chronic illnesses that include functional limitations and are particularly important during care transitions.

The population demands transparency, values immediacy and expects patient-centered care. Graduate medical education will be held accountable for outcomes, hospitals will become intensive care units and the healthcare system much more concerned with the continuum of care and efficient networks responsible for the care of the patient wherever the patient is located in the healthcare continuum. On the horizon looms the convenience of telehealth, online communication with physicians, electronic patient portals, and virtual visits. The US healthcare climate now focuses on cost avoidance, transforming this concept into a new cost center- indeed a profit center, which drives and rewards patient-centered care. This focus is unlikely to change, rather intensify as total spending on healthcare approaches 20% of the GDP. Changes in how healthcare is reimbursed and how physicians are paid will slowly but surely transform the healthcare system across the continuum of care.

This focus on value-based healthcare should also give hope to the field of Geriatrics. Value-based purchasing is a demand side strategy to reward quality in healthcare delivery. Effective healthcare services and high performing healthcare providers are incentivized to provide quality outcomes and to control costs. Geriatrics has always been a value-added program. Consider the possibilities of the futuristic healthcare team as a virtual team requiring Geriatric leadership and knowledge of care across the continuum. Consider care planning with hospitalists as part of the team. Hospitalists currently enjoy much support from hospital-based healthcare systems to efficiently treat and discharge patients admitted to high cost and intensive hospital beds. Hospitalists themselves however are poorly equipped to deal with continuity of care concerns and reduce repeat hospitalizations by themselves. Geriatrics involvement can enhance care. The inclusion of nursing home and home health personnel in team meetings to coordinate treatment, provide continuity of care and facilitate transitions of care could positively impact change of location for the patient. This paradigm shift can have enormous consequences to the field of Geriatrics, and to the healthcare system.

References

1. Sinsky C, Colligan L, Li L, Prgomet M, Reynolds S, Goeders L, Westbrook J, Tutty M, Blike G. Allocation of physician time and ambulatory practice: a time in motion study in 4 specialties. Ann Inter Med. 2016;165:753–60.
2. 2013 Health and Health Care of the Medicare Population. Table 2.1 Perceived Health and Functioning of Medicare Beneficiaries, by Age and by Gender and Age, 2. https://www.cms.gov/Research-Statistics-Data-and-Systems/Research/MCBS/Data-Tables-Items/2013HHC.html?DLPage=1&DLEntries=10&DLSort=0&DLSortDir=descending. Accessed 3 Apr 2017.
3. Table G. Current population reports- population projections of the United States by age, sex, race, and hispanic origin: 1995 to 2050. https://www.census.gov/prod/1/pop/p25-1130/p251130.pdf. Accessed 4 Apr 2017.
4. Alzheimer's Association. Alzheimer's disease facts and figures. 2017. Figure 4. http://www.alz.org/documents_custom/2017-facts-and-figures.pdf. Accessed 4 Apr 2017.

5. National Academies of Science, Engineering, and Medicine. Families caring for an aging America. www.nationalacademies.org/caregiving. Accessed 3 Apr 2017.
6. The Frameworks Institute. http://www.frameworksinstitute.org/aging.html. Accessed 3 Apr 2017.
7. Tinetti M. Mainstream or extinction: can defining who we are save geriatrics? J Am Geriatr Soc. 2016;64(7):1400–4.
8. Counsell SR, Callahan CM, Tu W, Stump TE, Arling GW. Cost analysis of the geriatric resources for assessment and care of elders care management intervention. J Am Geriatr Soc. 2009;57:1420–6.

Chapter 3
Incentives

Abstract Incentives are the currency of behavioral and organizational change. Incentives are generally classified under the headings of money and power, but they appear in a variety of guises. Incentives can be positive or negative, and are important influences on the process of change. The agent of change may not be able to control incentives, however it is imperative that the change agent be aware of the important incentives influencing decision-makers and those who control resources.

Incentives are the currency of behavioral and organizational change. The champion or agent of change often faces barriers and challenges to implementing new models and programs. Knowing which incentives are effective levers behind barriers is critical information for the change agent. For administrators and those in authority, incentives often take the form of power and money in many different forms. Incentives can be positive representing financial benefits and can be a huge motivation for behavior. Negative financial incentives may include punishment, fines, increased costs, regulatory constraints, and loss of reputation and market share. Many times incentives are created external to the institution and are influenced by regulations, laws, resource availability, and public expectations. Agents of change may not be able to control incentives, however they must respect and understand the important incentives influencing the decision-makers who control the resources required for the development of new models of care. Building a strategy or value proposition involves meeting common and overlapping objectives and also on arranging the incentives of those whose assistance is required. Occasionally reverse psychology may be required to address some barriers including withdrawal or withholding of services due to real or perceived concerns of the other party.

Power likewise can be a powerful incentive. Power is not inherently bad but is required to influence change. Power is necessary to acquire and direct resources in order to create new models and programs. Power can have negative consequences when individuals seek and use it for self-promotion. It is often readily apparent to others when power and control is utilized for the benefit of the individual, and not for the best interests of the program. Such individuals may create a close circle of advisors who resist new ideas from outsiders. Under these circumstances the agent of change may be seen as a threat. While the agent of change must recognize barriers

© Springer International Publishing AG 2017   11
J.S. Powers, *Creating a Value Proposition for Geriatric Care*, SpringerBriefs in
Health Care Management and Economics, DOI 10.1007/978-3-319-62271-2_3

created by powerful influences, even parties reluctant to collaborate may indeed cooperate when each can be useful to the other.

We now consider two examples of troublesome leadership strategies. How would you analyze the leadership style exemplified? How might leadership change if incentivized by different performance criteria or oversight?

Example 3.1 Living with Conflict I It was annual report time again and the section leaders for the division rarely spoke to each other. Work was done mainly in separate silos. While each program was academically strong, each was very different in focus with little integration. However under the guidelines of the grant, all sections were considered important although the program director clearly had favorite contributors, frequently devaluing the contributions of some sections, limiting resources, space, and personnel. It was apparent however that the granting administration highly valued these other components and the outcomes they produced. The director tolerated the contributions of the other sections, indeed depended on them and sometimes claimed credit for their efforts, because they were required contributions to the total output of the project.

Epilogue 3.1 Now the reader may reason, surely there is a better way. The author could not agree more. However it is important to realize the underlying motives behind the organization. The individual silos remain strong (and independent) without much need for direct involvement of the leader. Because of the productivity of the unit and the research funding it generates, the leadership behavior continues to be tolerated by the organization. It is what it is, and in fact, it works.

Example 3.2 Living with Conflict II Responding to an opportunity stemming from a mandate to form a new specialty program, a clinician abandoned prior commitments. Senior management was unresponsive to the concerns of ongoing program staff, refusing to provide alternate resources and even threatening to close the service. This produced increased workload and stress on the remaining clinicians. The clinical leader of the new program was very rigid and the interdisciplinary team members expressed many concerns about poor collaboration. The new program operated as a consultative service with little ownership of patients and no continuity with the primary care physicians. The program met benchmarking only one quarter in 4 years. A comparison program in the same region always met benchmark and exceeded stretch goals 3 out of the previous 4 years as well as exceeding the comparison site in 7 of 10 patient care domains. It also attracted many patients new to the system because of high patient and family satisfaction.

These two leaders in the preceding examples were left on their own with little oversight from senior leadership. Each had a relatively limited circle of professional supporters who were intensely loyal but hostile to outsiders. Both had allegations of intimidating behaviors leveled by staff. Colleagues interacting with each were resigned to tolerance and negotiating for overlapping needs, recognizing that collegial appearances were critical to maintaining relationships. Both leaders were subsequently passed over for promotions. Performance incentives that may have been beneficial could include colleague and staff evaluations, program performance and patient satisfaction ratings, as well as leadership coaching.

Sequel to 3.2 As the Geriatric program grew it was clear that resource sharing was inevitable, and that work load expectations would increase. The clinical leader of the new program had delegated many tasks to a small group of supporters and maintained control of scheduling and resources. Rather than relinquish control, all seemingly mutually beneficial proposals were rejected. A reverse psychology strategy involved a proposal for collaboration with shared workload in order to achieve mutual program objectives. As expected however the proposal was rejected, also forcing the individual to accept responsibility for increasing work-load productivity. Sometime later new leadership, responding to new performance objectives for the facility, placed this colleague in the situation of having to respond to poor quality metrics and performance. To address these gaps in care, they were placed on a committee to recommend improved identification of patients at risk for high resource utilization and providing appropriate management and care. The new leadership placed a priority on collaboration and benefits to the whole organization. The colleague was encouraged to utilize "shared" resources for the good of the entire program. Considering it their own new idea (positive frame affect) they promptly dropped all defenses and requested assistance in meeting these new challenges, finally permitting the crafting a program that combined all available resources to achieve the desired goal. We provide this as an example of a shift from an us-versus-them approach to a community working together in a common effort with shared resources to address gaps in care, for the betterment of the entire facility.

Knowledge of the motives affecting the decisions of essential players is critical to the change agent. External reviews, regulations and program guidelines are important levers of influence, often producing quick results when aligned with other performance goals. New performance objectives can be linked to support of new clinical programs that help administration and leadership meet these goals. Creating proposals with overlapping goals and program objectives valued by all participants is the task of the change agent. Understand the resources and priorities required and be willing to make compromises in order to achieve mutual goals. Demonstrating early successes helps achieve sustained cooperation in order to achieve greater outcomes together.

Example 3.3 Joining Forces to Achieve a Common End The Geriatric Service determined to join forces with two other small services in order to obtain an outpatient clinic program desired by all. Each service was too small to justify separate administrative support and space. However, together, a viable firm was formed to permit the growth of outpatient clinical services for each program. The Geriatric Service additionally required an interdisciplinary team and negotiated with Nursing, Pharmacy, and Social Work to obtain dedicated individuals, albeit with collateral duties, to participate part time in the clinical enterprise. In return the Geriatrics Program provided support to the institution for quality improvement committees, Joint Commission preparedness responsibilities, and care of complex patients.

For most proposals, a collaborative, win-win approach is recommended. This is the case where overlapping goals or job performance objectives overlap for all parties concerned. This cooperation is required to achieve a successful product, and helps to prioritize and direct the distribution of resources. It is well known in politics that most outcomes are achieved from working together, and that there are no permanent friends or permanent foes. Threats and brinkmanship can produce unintended consequences such as poor public impression and destroy future cooperation. This is especially important with programs having similar resource needs. Working together to produce a greater outcome may actually produce a mutually beneficial proposal.

The public has great individual expectations involving caregiver support, continuity of care, available and affordable health care, and a relationship with providers over time. They have a great incentive to advocate for Geriatrics and Primary Care program development. We need to cultivate and engage public support for Geriatrics, focus on caregiver needs, and exert political pressure to develop and enhance the programs which the public needs.

The rapid rise of the hospitalist profession is a good example of how professional and institutional incentives including defined work hours, efficient use of hospital resources, institutionalized handoffs, reduced reliance on the trainee workforce, and secure income have been valued by the healthcare profession and healthcare systems. This is however at odds with the expressed needs of the general public. Continuity of care is the Achilles heel of the hospitalist system. Why not harness the public's request for more primary care and continuity of care by further supporting graduate medical education to train more primary care providers and support them with lifestyle enhancements including interdisciplinary team care, improved communication, and interdisciplinary work skills? Communication and collaboration between levels of medical care, avoiding gaps in care during transitions, and accountability regarding return to higher levels of care should be shared among all components of the healthcare system in order to promote patient-centered, high-value care. Medical trainees likewise may be attracted to primary care if a team approach to the care of the patient and assistance from other healthcare professionals were part of the care model. These are strong incentives and include numerous elements for the agent of change to harness in order to promote change and new program development.

Is the authors' hope that these principles, the lessons learned, and the perspective gained from developing innovative value-based clinical programs for Universities and Government will inform the strategy of new change agents and also benefit the development of commercial healthcare business models as well.

Chapter 4
Strategies

Abstract Leadership involves advocating in the best interest of others. Leadership is about creating opportunity that is bigger than what might be created by oneself. Leadership is a function of expertise, change, risk, persistence, and trust. Leadership occurs at many different levels and comes in many different forms and different types of leadership require different skill sets. After instituting change the leader has to achieve a consensus for the value proposition and transfer ownership of responsibility for the program to the institution. This type of leadership requires a long-term perspective since change takes time and requires the presence of many enabling factors. Most administrators who control resources however have a very short-term perspective as a result of performance objectives and the need to respond to market forces. The change agent must learn to act strategically. This chapter is about leadership tools to act strategically.

This chapter is about strategies. The various circumstances and unique characteristics of each program being developed will require a different framework for planning and understanding change processes, particularly over an extended period of time. Many potential strategies are described below, and the change agent should feel free to choose whichever model best describes the circumstances and provides helpful strategic direction. They are not mutually exclusive models. On the contrary they are complementary and all have been useful at different times to the author in directing program development. These theories will be demonstrated in subsequent examples. The primary directive of the change agent is that the main purpose of the program is to benefit the institution.

Realize that there are numerous barriers to change and getting institutions to sustain and support new healthcare programs. The change agent's role consists of instituting a change, however small, demonstrating early gains, achieving a consensus or buy in of the value proposition, then transferring ownership of responsibility for the program to the institution for sustainment and growth (Fig. 4.1). The barriers to this process include vested interests which may suffer loss of resources, influence, or changes in the scope of their own program as a result of any change. Entrenched interests may have power or profit financially as a result of current systems and will understandably resist change. The agent of change must realize that even a well-articulated and justified proposal, while necessary, is not sufficient to

© Springer International Publishing AG 2017
J.S. Powers, *Creating a Value Proposition for Geriatric Care*, SpringerBriefs in
Health Care Management and Economics, DOI 10.1007/978-3-319-62271-2_4

Fig. 4.1 Role of the change agent

produce change. Goals and values are extremely important, but strategy is uniquely important. Strategy involves a process of instituting change including the formation of coalitions, the identification of complementary goals, the assessment of strengths and weaknesses, and the timing of the proposal. Strategy is extremely important to the process of implementation of any new program.

Consider the difference between immediate and long-term goals. The change agent must have a long term perspective, since change takes time and involves the creation and orchestration of many enabling factors. Most administrators, while well-intentioned, have very short-term perspectives as a result of competing performance objectives and the need to respond to immediate market forces. In our experience administrators often have a 2–5 year tenure. However interim administrators may have 6 months or 1 year terms. These may be brought in to institute unpopular changes, and then relocate. The change agent may benefit from waiting out regime changes, limiting losses, regrouping and reframing proposals at a later time with a more favorable administration. The forces of power and money are shifting to value-based purchasing and reimbursement models. Geriatric principles and innovations are increasing in importance and acceptance. The change agent must remain steadfast and patient. Reform takes time and changes are often incremental. Indeed, many reforms may even be too incremental to be immediately obvious.

Leadership is a function of: expertise, change, risk, persistence, and trust (Table 4.1). A wise man once said: "If people follow you, you're a leader." Physicians have great potential when they become involved as agents of change. Viewed as experts in healthcare matters, the public has a high regard for physicians and in fact looks to them for direction and leadership in matters involving health. In my experience, the public, government, and business as a rule, still defer to physicians as the healthcare experts. This acknowledgement not only pertains to personal health, but also includes policy arenas. Physician organizations are especially urged to provide input and guidance, helping to shape critical healthcare decisions.

Leadership can take many forms, but it is always personalized. And it is always about change. There is always one person, a leader, who begins anything. A leader possesses competency and engenders trust to create a shared context, inspiring others to work together to achieve common goals. This creates a structured support to guide transformation. Leadership involves risk tolerance, yes and persistence. A leader is motivated and passionate and ignites this in others. Some leaders lead by example and followers respond by imitation. Others facilitate shared leadership functions and provide advice to influence and enable changes at all levels.

Table 4.1 Leadership roles

Expertise
Change
Risk
Persistence
Trust

Although many seek leadership positions in order to influence change, in truth leadership occurs at many levels and different types of leadership require different skill sets. Some leaders create a membership-participatory organization style (bottom-up leadership) rather than a top-down environment. These leaders contribute experience to influence decision making and are foundational for building a culture of quality and safety. Their influence is critical in creating measurable objectives and work plans leading to system-wide changes. They may initiate activities voluntarily and function in acting roles, creating new positions for others. Informal leadership roles do not always provide official recognition, so these agents of change often possess a selfless dedication. But all are leaders.

Professional schools are full of high achievers with impressive credentials and affable personalities. One trait however which separates the great from the good is humility: the ability to give credit to others, and to show appreciation. True leaders are more concerned about the well-being of those around them than they are about themselves. Leadership involves advocating for the best interest of others. It's not about having people work for you or leveraging other people's talents to make your life easier, or for personal gain. Leadership is about creating opportunity that is bigger than what might be created by oneself. It involves organizing others to work with you. It involves evaluating decisions based on how they will improve the lives of others.

Leaders have a clear vision with a discipline and commitment to work for change. They frame the issues and give a sense of scale, engaging others in causes bigger than themselves. Authentic leaders are competent and personally trustworthy. They are good communicators, building relationships through empathy, understanding, and inspiration. An inclusive leadership style acknowledges others' values and points of view, and energizes them to create a committed action. While the mind weighs facts, the heart seeks meaning, and the effective leader manages both to give meaning and relevance to the cause for change.

Many true leaders are conferred leaders, acknowledged either formally or informally for their competence and experience and consulted for their expertise to guide the discussion, both formally and informally. They stimulate and support the planning, implementation, and evaluation of change processes. These agents of change form a foundation for building a culture of quality and safety, complementing existing organizational structures. A responsible organization ignores their sound advice at its own peril. Many physicians adopt executive and administrative responsibilities, but may not be recognized as executives. Not all leaders are in charge of institutional levers, nor appointed by others in authority.

Becoming involved as a physician leader includes volunteering for quality improvement and safety committees. It involves accepting appointments to hospital, organization, and practice boards. Familiarity with organizational performance metrics and outcomes measures is also critical prerequisites for articulating strategies to move organizations. Opportunities to institute change are often unpredictable. It is an axiom that success comes to those who have prepared sound plans and who take advantage of opportunities as they develop. Opportunities may be time-limited, may be timed to the initiation of new leadership, occur as a consequence of new policies strategic goals or external events, or complementary to new priorities which need to be assessed and acted on by the agent of change. Indeed, the agent of change realizes that there are many PDSA (Plan Do Study and Act) improvement cycles of organizational development and process improvement. Harnessing the proposal for a new program development or model of care to PDSA improvement cycles facilitates strategy and positions the change agent to plan accordingly Fig. 4.1).

Focus on achievable outcomes and early successes when introducing a program. Early demonstrations may need to be part-time in nature. All proposals will involve collaborators and other resources. Obtain information on the incentives and motives of others that might be included both as collaborators and those who may pose barriers to implementation of the project. Be sure to engage partners and allow for some ownership of overlapping goals and needs. Check on the progress towards the goal and lessons learned and then adapt the process and strategy required to progress towards the goal. Plan the next step revising goals with new approaches and even new partners.

The agent of change will be faced with challenges and barriers and will need to be creative as many responses will be unscripted, perhaps even pushing one out of their comfort zone. The following is a list of leadership strategies which the author has used to solve problems and overcome barriers to program development (Table 4.2).

Promote the program as a solution to gaps in care which will appeal to additional audiences as sources of support. This strategy grows supporters over time. Meet with and seek higher administrative authorities if available and seek their influence and willingness to act on behalf of the program. These additional supporters can be invaluable in addressing program barriers, individual reservations, and garnering

Table 4.2 Leadership strategies

Obtain new sources of support
Appeal to higher authority
Employ group strategies
Obtain information on incentives and motives of key players
Let others speak positively on your behalf
Continuously build the program as a resource for all, avoiding personal gain

further support. Always act on behalf of the institution. Employ group strategy with open and transparent meetings, stressing long-term goals and marketing the program as a resource to benefit all. Obtain information on the incentives of key actors their concerning their motives and self-interest. This information is critical for both supporters as well as those who might pose as barriers. Some of these incentives may be performance objectives including cost avoidance, a desire for space or new program funding, meeting educational requirements and needs of trainees, responding to external regulations, enhancement of quality indicators and patient satisfaction. Encourage advocates to speak in support of the proposal. Newcomers in authority can be especially influential as they often have a honeymoon period and they lack a history of involvement with potential antagonists. Supporters may even reflect their own self-interest, if it helps further program development. This broadens the base of support and minimizes personal focus on the agent of change. Promoting the benefits of the program for the institution as a resource for all provides the most stable and sustainable form of support.

The PARIHS (Promoting Action on Research Implementation in Health Services) framework is a useful model to guide implementation [1] (Table 4.3). Implementation processes commonly include planning, engaging support, executing, reflecting, and evaluating.

Strategies for a successful change implementation can also be explained by the Four Stage Model for organizational stages of change (Modern Organizational Theory) [2]. These consist of awareness, identification, implementation, and institutionalization (Table 4.4). Awareness includes educating management about gaps in care and the opportunities to improve care by the adoption of new models. Identification includes naming key personnel, best practices, and outlining the new model of care. Implementation involves a strategy for introducing the new program, demonstrating early successes for all stakeholders, and a time line for full operation. Institutionalization involves sustainment of the program by leadership, planned regular review of outcome metrics and quality indicators, and transfer of ownership to the institution.

Table 4.3 Implementation process

Planning
Engaging support
Executing
Reflecting
Evaluating

Table 4.4 Organizational change

Awareness
Identification
Implementation
Institutionalization

Table 4.5 Kotter's 8-step framework

1.	Create a sense of urgency
2.	Pull together the guiding team
3.	Develop the change in vision and strategy
4.	Communicate for understanding and buy-in
5.	Empower others to act
6.	Promote short-term wins
7.	Don't let up
8.	Create a new culture

The PARIHS framework and Modern Organizational Theory are helpful for understanding the development of new programs. (*See* ***Example 9.2*** *Enhancing Accountability, p. 47.*) This process involved standardizing a long term care inspection process, as a result of criticisms for previous lack of oversight. Public criticism brought the administration to the awareness stage in the modern organizational scheme. The identification phase included the first two components of the PARIHS framework, a careful planning for change by engaging support from content experts and frontline staff and committing required resources to the effort. The implementation phase took 2 years with reflection on the process and involvement of all stakeholders through a modified Delphi approach. Following implementation of the inspection process, all stakeholders continue to be involved in the evaluation and continued process improvement of the model. Institutionalization, the final stage of the modern organizational scheme included scheduled regional meetings and report to senior leadership to review quality indicators, also providing peer support and mentorship for the inspection teams.

Kotter's Eight-Step Framework for Institutional Change can also be very helpful in building strategy for change (Table 4.5) [3]. This framework provides additional strategic insight and the eight stages can be demonstrated within the modern organizational schema as: (a) (Steps 1 & 2) Setting the stage, creating a sense of urgency and pulling together a guiding team, (b) (Step 3) Deciding what to do–developing the change in vision and strategy, (c) (Steps 4–7) Make it happen. This consists of communicating an understanding and buy-in. It includes sharing control and empowering others to act, promoting short-term wins to demonstrate progress to all stakeholders, and being persistent – don't give up. And D) (Step 8) Make it stick by creating a new culture to sustain the program. Foster ownership by the organization by marketing the benefits of the program to the institution. Consider **Example 6.1** (p. 32) and **Epilogue 8.2** (p. 42), *A Good Model Catches On*. A Geriatric Evaluation and Management Unit started out small with few resources. It built on initial successes and always remained helpful to the administration. The marketing strategy included educating clinicians and other supporters, and obtaining buy-in from the administration. Operations data demonstrated that the program provided excellent clinical outcomes consistently over a 15 year period. At a critical time, culture

Table 4.6 Negotiating

Interest-based negotiation ~90%
Create value for both sides
Strategy is open
Positional negotiation ~10%
Perceived winners and losers
Use of tactics

change occurred and cost avoidance and population-based performance measures dominated administrative attention. The care model was ready to seize the opportunity and with additional support and growth came to help the entire institution achieve new value-based performance objectives.

Selling to management involves making an effective and compelling business case. The CEO wants to know what is different (wrong or needed, or gaps in care) and clear concrete suggestions and solutions (what is the value added)? Interest-based negotiation creates value for both sides. Value-based care is exemplified by the Triple Aim of the Institute of Medicine [4]: (1) Improved the care experience for the patient, (2) Improved quality of care, and (3) Cost effective care (including cost avoidance). How can we harness the population demands for primary care, value, and continuity of care in order to create value for all?

For most proposals, a collaborative, win-win approach is recommended (Table 4.6). This is where overlapping goals and performance objectives among all stakeholders come together to achieve a successful program. The approach also creates order and prioritizes the distribution of resources. The most positive outcomes are often achieved by working together, producing greater and more permanent results. Collaboration is especially important when potentially competing programs have similar resource needs.

The use of tactics such as threats, creation of barriers, and creating negative impressions of other parties often has unintended consequences in terms of poor relationships, distrust, isolation, and poor public image. Changing market forces, regulations, and new performance objectives may then place the parties in a difficult position regarding future support and collaboration. Scarce resources may not be effectively shared, to the detriment of all concerned.

The PDSA cycles for quality improvement (Fig. 4.2 – from *Management Matters: Building Enterprise Capability* by John Hunter [5]) is an important tool that can be used to frame the process of change. Originally conceived to understand and improve processes of care and quality of care, the PDSA Improvement Cycle can be used to further refine strategies for change. (P) stands for Plan, identifying the metrics or theory. (D) stands for Do, or implementation. (S) stands for Study of the outcomes and includes a reality check on the success or failures of programs. (A) stands for Act, adjusting the goal based on learning over the prior cycle. Each of the elements of the PDSA Improvement Cycle have different time frames. A project may be many years in the planning phase "P" before it can be field tested. Many

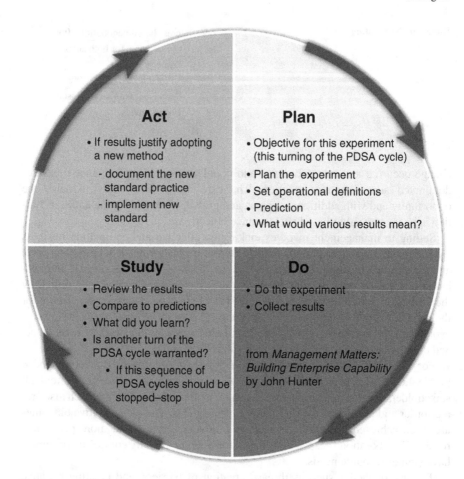

Fig. 4.2 PDSA improvement cycle (Figure reproduced by permission https://curiouscat.com/management/dictionary/pdsa. Accessed February 17, 2017)

enabling factors and conditions may have to be met and the timing of the launch strategically planned to optimize success. The field test or launch of the project "D" is critically important. Early successes need to be seen in order to guarantee continued support and resources. The project needs to be critically assessed "S" in terms of implementation experience, early outcomes, and trends. Depending on this assessment a new direction, new features or new support might be required, giving rise to the next phase of the cycle "A."

PDSA improvement cycles can help explain the processes of change and demonstrate gaps and barriers. Even the best plans meet resistance in the face of real world realities and require modification. In our experience the development of new programs takes many years. New programs and the sustainment of ongoing programs require resources and approval from leadership. There is a continued need to reassess strategies, particularly in the face of changing leadership, in order to develop and sustain new programs and models of care.

Table 4.7 PDSA strategic work chart

Stage	Description	Steps
Plan	What is the goal?	What is the strategy?
	1.	1.
	2.	2.
	3.	3.
Do	Aim for small successes	Initiate (pilot), observe responses
	1.	1.
	2.	2.
	3.	3.
Study (check)	Check outcomes	Reflect on lessons learned
	1.	1.
	2.	2.
	3.	3.
Act	Refine the goal	Modify the strategy, consider new resources
	1.	1.
	2.	2.
	3.	3.

Table 4.8 SMART processes

Specific
Measurable
Attainable
Relevant
Time- bound

We utilized PDSA improvement cycles in *Example 3.2* (p. 12) and **Sequel 5.**1 *Living with Conflict (p. 39).* The initial strategy was one of cooperation. However, that failed due to a perceived need to control by the other parties involved. The strategy then shifted to one of challenging the other party to accept responsibility. Over a 3-year period, culture change occurred based on value-based performance objective goals, permitting a renewed strategy of cooperation to permit shared resources to achieve common quality performance objectives. A sample PDSA strategic work chart is displayed in Table 4.7 to help illustrate the process.

We introduce a final strategy for change agents – the SMART process application [6]. Introduced by Doran to facilitate organizational change. Successful goals should be: Specific, Measurable, Attainable, Relevant, and Time–bound (Table 4.8). By focusing on specific goals and outcomes and measuring progress toward attainment of the specific goal. Even very slow incremental changes can be seen as building blocks on the past to developing large integrated programs. We utilized this model in building the VA Geriatric outpatient program (Geri-PACT) as detailed in *Example 5.2 Patients Vote with their Feet (p. 28),* and *Sequel 7.1* (p. 38).

References

1. Rycroft-Malone J. The PARIHS framework–a framework for guiding the implementation of evidence–based practice. J Nurs Care Qual. 2004;19:297–304.
2. Steckler A, Goodman R, Kegler MC. Mobilizing organizations for health enhancement: theories of organizational change. In: Glanz K, Rimer BK, Lewis FM, editors. Health behavior and health education: theory, research and practice. 3rd ed. San Francisco: Jossey-Bass; 2002. p. 335–60.
3. Kotter J. Our iceberg is melting. London: Penguin Press; 2016.
4. Institute of Medicine (U.S.). Crossing the quality chasm: a new health system for the 21st century. Washington, DC: National Academy Press; 2001.
5. Hunter J. Management matters: building enterprise capability. Victoria: Lean Publishing; 2013. C 2012–2013 John Hunter https://leanpub.com/managementmatters. Accessed 17 Feb 2017.
6. Doran GT. There's a S.M.A.R.T. way to write management's goals and objectives. Management review. AMA Forum. 1981;70(11):35–6.

Chapter 5
Development of VA Geriatrics Programs

Abstract The Veterans Administration has had a large and credible influence on the development of Geriatrics as a field in the United States. Generally within the Veterans Health Administration, service needs align with the finances and program delivery to meet performance objectives and accountability within a single payer system. Responding to accountability to the public following a 2014 failure to provide access to primary care, contributed to by falsified reports and a flawed incentive system, a large portion of VA leadership was replaced and given new quality performance metrics: SAIL, the Strategic Analytics for Improvement and Learning Value Model. Many VA hospitals achieved remarkably low ratings, and new managers have been put on notice to improve quality through value-based healthcare transformation. These managers are listening to potential Geriatric care models which help them achieve these objectives.

The VA has long had an interest in Geriatrics beginning as early as 1975 with the development of the Geriatric Research Education and Clinical programs (GRECC) partly as a response to a growing number of elderly WW2 Veterans. These geriatric resource centers, along with affiliated universities, served as a base for the development of Geriatrics as a field in the United States. At our own University affiliate, the development of the GRECC stimulated initiation of a Geriatrics fellowship program for physicians to obtain further training in the field.

Generally, within the Veterans Health Administration, the service needs align with the finances and program delivery to meet performance objectives and accountability as a single payer system. The VA is responsible to the public but depends on congressional support, and is subject to budgetary fluctuations.

The Veterans Millennium Healthcare and Benefits Act of 1999 enhanced the provision of extended care services to veterans, and is sometimes called the Mill Bill or the Medicare for Veterans Act. It firmly established that the Department of Veterans Affairs (VA) should accord the highest priority for nursing home care to the most severely disabled veterans and those needing care for service-connected disabilities. It also ensured that veterans enrolled in the VA health care system receive non-institutional, extended-care services, including geriatric evaluations and adult day health care. It mandated and funded the establishment of numerous non-institutional care programs including adult day health, contract nursing home, homemaker home

© Springer International Publishing AG 2017

J.S. Powers, *Creating a Value Proposition for Geriatric Care*, SpringerBriefs in Health Care Management and Economics, DOI 10.1007/978-3-319-62271-2_5

25

health services, and home-based primary care as essential elements of veterans healthcare. Veterans may choose to utilize private insurance, Medicare, or VA benefits, and in any standard metropolitan statistical area (SMSA) some 15–30% of Veterans may utilize VA benefits. Veterans and Medicare benefits can be complementary, but neither permits duplication of the same services.

Many parts of the country were deficient in the provision of veterans' geriatrics and home and community-based services, particularly in the Southeast. This region of the country had the lowest utilization of many of these healthcare services and some the highest severity of disease ratings, as measured by Medicare as well as VA standards. When our region was awarded a GRECC, it was incumbent on the Clinical Director to assist in the development of these geriatric and non-institutional care resources for the Southeast.

The implementation technique chosen by the clinical director was primarily educational, providing content expertise to assist facility directors and managers to understand the provisions of the Mill Bill, also explaining the concept behind the geriatric models of care which they were asked to initiate at their facilities. Personal visits to each facility greatly facilitated the planning and implementation timeline required to enable the development of the non-institutional care resources. A Regional Council, chaired by the GRECC Clinical Director, provided peer support and best practice education for facility personnel involved in non-institutional care program development and administration. The Council eliminated administrative barriers to program development and fostered a collaboration among facilities which continues to exist and has facilitated the development of many additional new programs. Facility directors responded to the Council's recommendations and between 2000 and 2005 developed many of the recommended non-institutional care resources, meeting and often exceeding facility targets. In 2005 The Council developed Home-Based Primary Care, a VA interdisciplinary care team for homebound older adults. It followed in 2008 with a long-awaited launch of sorely needed hospice and palliative care services in our area. In its first year, some 30% of hospice enrollees were found to utilize their VA benefits for the first time. In 2010 Geriatric and Extended Care (GEC) Service Chiefs were installed at all major facilities, and in 2015 finally extended to our own facility. In 2011 a geriatric primary care patient aligned care team (Geri-PACT) was initiated. This patient centered medical home model dramatically reduced hospitalizations and polypharmacy. Due to its early successes the model was funded by the Regional Office and made mandatory at all regional facilities in 2016.

Fueled by incentives to minimize wait lists, the VA had an access crisis in 2014 related to falsified data regarding primary care access, confirmed by the Office of the Inspector General (OIG). The Secretary of Veterans Affairs took early retirement, and the VA Director resigned. After an initial stopgap funding to increase access in 2015, Congress withheld a $15 billion continuation plan for facility access funding in fiscal year 2016, stressing efficiency and value–based care, while increasing funds for non-VAChoice contract services for veterans residing at greater distances from VA facilities. This translated into an approximately $15 million deficit for each major VA facility, producing a wholesale exodus of administrators. By some accounts as many as 40% of leadership was replaced or left the system. New personal were given new quality performance metrics known as SAIL [1].

SAIL, the Strategic Analytics for Improvement and Learning Value Model, is a web-based, balanced scorecard model that the Department of Veterans Affairs developed to measure, evaluate, and benchmark quality and efficiency internally at its medical centers. There are nine SAIL domains: Performance measures, Satisfaction, Mortality, Length of Stay, Access, Efficiency, Ambulatory Care Sensitive Condition Hospitalizations, and Avoidable Adverse Events. These metrics fostered new alliances with clinical leaders to achieve common objectives at VA facilities.

Our experience is that reform sometimes requires a little embarrassment. Prior to the Mill Bill, our region of the country was a low performer in many geriatric spheres. Despite the production of numerous executive decision memos benchmarking our performance against national trends, the regional director remained unmoved. We learned, however that being embarrassed at national meetings and conferences can be an effective strategy when combined with personal family experiences.

Example 5.1 When It's Personal, It Becomes Important Our Network Director did not believe in hospice and palliative care despite numerous meetings encouraging his support, recommendations of the Joint Commission, and the presence of funding opportunities to encourage development of the program. Nurses and physicians concerned about end of life care volunteered their efforts but without any administrative support. The region was often criticized at national meetings because of its low performance in the area of advanced disease processes. It was only after the director's mother developed breast cancer and received hospice services herself that he was convinced that it was a good program. When he returned from his mother's funeral he apologetically said to all of us that he had been wrong and that he now supported the development of the program. A short time later, new VA directives required the development of hospice and palliative care services at all facilities.

There are many barriers to the development of government programs including lack of ownership of the program, changing leadership and changing priorities. Waiting for administrative mandates to develop programs tends to be a top-down process, with slow responses to directives, and funding may be delayed. Administrators may change every 2–5 years. The agent of change may sometimes have to endure an unresponsive or hostile administration with hope for a more receptive new administration. Our experience has been that with change comes opportunity – development of new programs may be more accepted by incoming management providing greater opportunities to advance and develop new models of care.

In example that follows, how would the reader respond to patient requests for outpatient care? Asking permission to create an outpatient clinic was sure to evoke a prompt negative response from administration. There appeared to be no chance for buy-in, so the agent of change proceeded to use resources at hand and proceed to pilot a small clinic in response to patient demands.

Example 5.2 Patients Vote with Their Feet The demand for outpatient services was so intense due to inadequate primary care resources, that patients would often show up on the hospital floor from which they had been discharged asking for follow-up care, prescription refills, and paperwork completion for benefits and services. In order to respond to patient requests, they were escorted to a vacant room on the hospital floor with temporary signs posted. During an internal inspection, the facility director discovered the clinic room, became incensed and reiterated his resolution to never have a clinic facility. He personally removed the signs, stopping them on the floor! Within the next year however new directives mandated the development of primary care and outpatient services, and the director was transferred to another facility. Outpatient resources continue to be developed throughout the VA system, with the demand greatly exceeding expectations, forcing the VA to rush to accommodate these new requests and to diminish waiting times. (Sequel … Example 7.1, p. 38)

While no new resources were given to start the clinic, initial successes based on patient satisfaction placed the part-time clinic in a strategically strong position to assist new leadership to respond to new institutional performance objectives. By keeping the clinic structure intact, it became relatively easy to expand the clinic as new space and full-time personnel were provided by a new administration in order to achieve performance goals.

Managers are guided by a number of incentives including specific performance objectives, number of unique veterans served, wait lists, clinical and financial outcomes, and the cost effectiveness of specific programs. They are also interested in the impact of new programs on existing programs, either off-setting costs, improving outcomes or relieving demand. If a program can demonstrate positive outcomes, in our experience it generally is sustained. The VA has been a leader in the development of many new models of care including telemedicine, computerized video-telemedicine, and team-based care. It was one of the first healthcare systems to develop an electronic medical record, electronic patient portals, and to provide disease-state management. All primary care is now delivered as a Patient Aligned Care Teams (PACT) [2, 3], a patient-centered medical home with full supporting staff, leading the way for other healthcare systems to revitalize primary care services (see Chap. 7).

References

1. VA Sail Metrics. http://www.va.gov/QUALITYOFCARE/measure-up/SAIL_definitions.asp. Accessed 13 Feb 2017.
2. Department of Veterans Affairs, Veterans Health Administration. Patient Aligned Care Team (PACT) Handbook, Washington, DC; 2014. https://www.va.gov/VHAPUBLICATIONS/ViewPublication.asp?pub_ID=2977. Accessed 23 Mar 2017.
3. Bodenheimer T, Grumbach K. Improving primary care: strategies and tools for a better practice. (UCSF Primary Care). New York: McGraw-Hill; 2007. ISBN paperback 9780071447386.

Chapter 6
Development of University Geriatrics Programs

Abstract The provision of lucrative, procedure-based specialty care has influenced the care delivery model and business plan for medical care in the United States for many decades. Conversely there has been less emphasis on Geriatrics and Primary Care. Graduate Medical Education likewise has provided little support for the development of geriatrics training. Universities as well as the commercial sector have to respond to the financial realities accompanying a change to value-based purchasing in healthcare. Universities are reluctant to change old business models, however there is great opportunity to collaborate with colleagues in hospital medicine and administration in applying geriatric principles to advance the delivery of medical care as well as medical education. Graduate medical education will be held accountable for outcomes demand by the public. A revitalized team-based primary care could help reverse the trend towards specialization among medical graduates and increase the appeal of primary care practice to generations of physicians, adding to enhanced access and quality of care for patients.

Johns Hopkins and UCLA were early adopters in creating geriatric programs. Currently most of the 149 United States medical schools provide required geriatric training. In some centers Geriatrics is a department unto itself. In most however it is a division within the Internal Medicine Department. A number of other organizational structures include Sections of Geriatrics within Family Medicine or General Internal Medicine Divisions.

Universities as well as the commercial sector have to respond to the financial realities accompanying a change to value base purchasing in the healthcare sector. But universities must also operate with a focus on education. This educational emphasis is an ever present overlay on all aspects of a university healthcare system. Previous emphasis on specialty care and training, funded by NIH training grants has created excellent specialty care in the United States which is the envy of the world. The provision of lucrative, procedure-based specialty care has influenced the care delivery model and business plan for medical care in the United States for many decades. Conversely there is been less emphasis on Geriatrics, Primary Care, transitions of care, and home and community-based services.

Graduate Medical Education likewise has provided little support for the development of Geriatrics training. University hospitals and educational institutions value

© Springer International Publishing AG 2017

J.S. Powers, *Creating a Value Proposition for Geriatric Care*, SpringerBriefs in Health Care Management and Economics, DOI 10.1007/978-3-319-62271-2_6

differences, diversity, advancement of knowledge, and exposure of students and trainees to the newest ideas. But they are also influenced by financing and reimbursement. Specialty programs have been emphasized historically so trainees in primary care fields must complete on a very uneven playing field at the institutional level for indirect Medicare education funding.

Opportunities for training support for Geriatrics and Primary Care however are changing as the healthcare system emphasizes efficiency and quality of care and with changing incentives created by a value-based healthcare transformation, and value – based payment models. [1] Collaboration between community partners is being emphasized particularly to reduce complications related to poor transitions of care and to minimize costly repeat hospitalizations. There is also competition among hospital systems in the same locality for the regional recognition of being designated the preferred provider by patients and employers.

Trainees also realize the need for experience in caring for complex older adults. At our institution it was the students who first requested the opportunity to experience the nursing home environment. Consequently a teaching nursing home program was initiated. Additional requests from residents stimulated a geriatrics clinic to provide consultation and outpatient management for complex patients with advanced disease processes. The hospital likewise requested assistance in the development of a long-term acute care unit (LTAC) to assist with placements and to reduce the acute care length of stay. While relatively few physician trainees enter the field of geriatrics, trainees recruited from within their own institutions have tended to be committed to growing local geriatric programs and to remain at their institutions. For all physician trainees who undergo required geriatric training, the goal of making them good geriatricians for their own patients has been well accepted, as most realize the benefits of learning to care for medically complex older adults as helpful toward their future specialty orientation.

There is hope however as increasing numbers of grants for interdisciplinary education and diseases impacting geriatric care–those things that the public demands–have stimulated other departments to collaborate with Geriatrics in order to be competitive for funding. Collaborations between Ophthalmology, Orthopedics, Psychiatry, Neurology, Emergency Medicine, Oncology, Cardiology, and Geriatrics are good examples. Specialty trainees have come to appreciate the value of medical research and educational funding for aging concerns. Our own Geriatric program has received valuable input from colleagues in specialties funded for cross – disciplinary research and education.

At our University, grateful families were extremely important in the creation of a Chair in Geriatrics. Following a 20 year long enabling period with the development of some 20 different geriatric educational and clinical models and sites of care, in 2006 a family donated funds for a Chair in Aging on behalf of a former medical school graduate. The University created a Center on Aging with a research Chair for Quality in Aging. The Center on Aging became a place for many young investigators to discuss and review findings and also receive encouragement and mentorship. Within this framework many new educational and research grants were obtained including the Reynolds Foundation, Beeson Career Development Awards, Geriatric

Education Centers (GEC – HRSA), NIH, and CMS Innovation Grants, greatly strengthening geriatrics research and education at the medical school and postgraduate level.

Approximately 10 years later an additional chair was donated by the family of another former medical school graduate, a practicing physician in the community who developed Alzheimer's disease and was cared for by the University Geriatrics Program. This chair was dedicated to Alzheimer's research and formed the basis for an academic Division of Geriatrics within the Department of Internal Medicine.

In our experience the development of a separate geriatric division is important to facilitate program growth. There are potentially many competing priorities when Geriatrics is buried in the administration of a large General Medicine or Family Medicine Department. The strategy for the development of a Division of Geriatrics required a 30 year-long courtship of slow but steady growth of educational, clinical, and research programs to obtain grateful family support. Throughout that time frame, we were fortunate that changes in administration which occurred on average every 5–10 years demonstrated an incremental increase in acceptance of geriatrics as a credible field.

Program development included development of an Acute Care for Elderly (ACE) inpatient teaching service [2], a geriatrics clinic which served many additional faculty families, a teaching nursing home, a palliative care service, and support for numerous hospital programs including Joint Commission preparedness, interdisciplinary team training, Falls Prevention and Skin Care Committees, expert content guidance for initiation of a home health agency, and a hospital – wide geriatric consult service. The Geriatrics Program also provided required geriatric training for residents and accepted hospital patients in transfer to reduce excessive caseloads for Internal Medicine residents, helping to maintain the residency program accreditation. Growth of Geriatrics contributed content expertise to the development of the Geriatric Psychiatry Program and its associated fellowship. It also supported other university programs concerned with aging representing diverse fields such as Engineering, the Arts, and a Humanities – based narrative history program.

There is an incentive for university hospitals to affiliate with VA facilities which provide faculty support to the academic affiliate. This was the case with our Geriatric Research Education and Clinical (GRECC) Program which provided 12 FTEE physician positions, greatly assisting the further development of our university geriatrics program. It also increased collaboration with colleagues in biomedical and quality improvement research fields akin to geriatrics who had overlapping interest and goals, facilitating new funding opportunities, career development awards, and educational programs.

The Geriatric Program instituted the first interdisciplinary team-based care using an autonomy supportive functional model [3]. That is, all team members function at the top of their license, challenging each to perform at the highest level to collaborate and to develop creative solutions to the numerous issues involved in the care of complex patients. This model is based on the self-determination theory of team function [4–6], creating an autonomy-supportive climate where individuals are motivated to work together with other team members to achieve improved patient

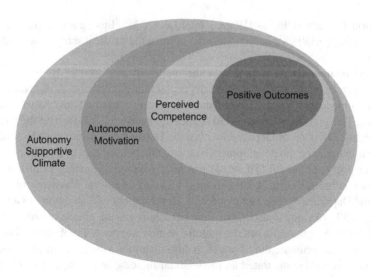

Fig. 6.1 Self-determination model of team function

outcomes (Fig. 6.1). The geriatric team was interdisciplinary in composition and function. Harmonious differences were valued and the primary group task was improved patient outcome and leadership was task-dependent.

The development of a team approach to care was of great importance to the University, although this was not initially apparent. *(Epilogue ... Example 8.1, p. 41)*

Example 6.1 Politics Is Everywhere-Persistence Pays Off While still in its developing phase, the Geriatric Program, administratively located within the Division of General Medicine, operated some 20 sites of care and provided inpatient, outpatient, and consultative services through which internal medicine residents and geriatric fellows rotated. The program remained vigorous despite a meager staff of 5 faculty, with little institutional support. During a hospital floor renovation and turnover of 1 physician involved the Geriatric Service; the administration determined that a growing hospitalist program better deserved the faculty position, as well as the team room dedicated to the Geriatric Service. The service might have closed the program and contracted the provision of vital services. Instead, for several years the remaining geriatrics faculty assumed additional call and subdivided a faculty office to function as a team room in order to preserve the program. Fellowship funding, accreditation, and workload were maintained because of the service needs. This helped to justify the program. Eventually, a new Chief of Staff and Quality Management officer were appointed. Finally at approximately the 4 year mark the same Administrative Chief we had denied resources was placed on a committee to improve the efficiency of hospital care, particularly the elderly with multiple chronic conditions. Under the direction of the new Chief Quality Officer he quickly realized the importance of the Geriatric Team and helped facilitate the allocation of resources, which included expanded team membership, cohorting of patient rooms, additional faculty, assistance with coverage, and provision of meeting space. The Geriatric Inpatient Service now is an accepted fixture intimately involved in the hospital's mission. (Sequel ... Example 8.2, p. 42)

It would have been easy for the agent of change to respond negatively to the loss of resources, succumbing to a short-term administrative goal. We caution not to burn bridges although it may be tempting. Avoiding making a disappointing event into a personal vendetta, although it may feel like such. It is important to maintain relationships. Previous opponents may be needed to support future proposals. Seek allies in related fields, such as QM. They are potential collaborators, and may be instrumental in helping to help change.

Once formed, the Division of Geriatrics was structurally a great help in advancing program development. Program development often proceeded in spite of the administration and required a grass roots strategy of finding and developing its own resources, as opposed to a top-down supportive approach with up-front funding. At a University Medical Center physician leaders in academics are often appointed on the basis of research achievements, funding success, or educational skills and accomplishments, not necessarily for clinical strengths or clinical program development experience. However, these appointed leaders frequently need the assistance of other faculty colleagues to support clinical programs. Agents of change may not be given leadership positions, indeed may need to step back and sustain the program with many volunteer clinical hours, call and coverage in order to support training venues and convince the University to assume ownership, refine and adapt the clinical and educational programs, and hire additional clinical faculty and staff to support these resources. The change agent's reward is the similar to that of the educator: the gratification of seeing the mentor's influence persist in the programs and individuals they formed and sustained.

The agent of change will potentially receive little recognition locally while developing a program utilizing a grass-roots approach. Sharing strategies while meeting with colleagues at national conferences can provide an important support group. Building on small successes, embracing new clinical paradigms, and supporting colleagues in other fields where interests overlap are also successful sustainment strategies.

CMS has challenged health systems to focus on value-based healthcare transformation and payment models as opposed to fee for service and volume profit. University hospitals have previously relied on a successful strategy of specialty training emphasizing procedure-based specialty care. This has been extremely profitable and has advanced the science of Medicine in many ways. Universities are reluctant to change this business model, however, funding, alternative payment models, and changes in the regulatory environment are potent levers for institutional change (see Chap. 9). Geriatric principles are critical in negotiating and thriving in this new healthcare environment. Indeed many health systems are borrowing Geriatric concepts and taking credit for applying geriatric principles to their management. There is great opportunity to collaborate with colleagues in hospital medicine and administration in refining the application of geriatric principles to meet local market needs. In this changing environment, the mission of the agent of change is to identify who is in charge of programs that can utilize geriatric input and to provide clear and concrete solutions with produce mutual benefits.

Consider this proposal to revitalize primary care resident education with outpatient team- based care. Value-based healthcare purchasing and the systemic changes it produces has the potential to provide many long term benefits to society and medical practice. It represents an enormous opportunity to advance the delivery of medical care as well as medical education [1]. Barriers to accepting Geriatrics and geriatric models of care currently include professional uncertainty, lack of training, and lack of skills to appreciate, understand and embrace a new paradigm for medical culture change. There is also a lack of high-quality evidence of model program effectiveness and lack of financial incentives under fee for service.

Currently there aren't enough primary care physicians to fill societies' need. However, teams of nurse practitioners and physician assistants working collaboratively with physicians can do so. What if our training of medical students and residents included a team-based model for primary care to prepare them for clinical practice in the twenty-first century? Consider a practice model of several advanced practice nurses or physician assistants seeing patients in the same outpatient setting as a primary care physician. Nurses or physician assistants functioning as billing providers could see 80% or more of routine patients, utilizing protocols and evidence-based guidelines. Physicians seeing more complex patients such as those with co-morbidities, could serve as consultants regarding non-responders, determining diagnostic testing strategies, and deciding on complex therapies, hospitalization, and referrals. Care managers utilizing electronic medical records to assist with chronic disease management could create a patent centered medical home model for appropriate patients. Affiliation with selected disease specialists could extend the model to a medical neighborhood.

A team-based primary care model could function as an innovative training site for residents and students and provide opportunities to demonstrate ACGME Core Competencies [7] (Table 6.1) in the following unique ways:

Developing a team based primary care model will take effort to overcome established physician incentives and practice styles designed for fee for service models. Establishing billing provider roles for advanced practice nurses and physician assistants at teaching hospitals will be challenging. Protocols to treat the majority of illnesses will need to be adapted and periodically updated [8]. There will be initial salary costs, care manager positions, and non-billable team meeting time that will need to be covered. Space for care managers and conferences will need to be accommodated. New practices roles for physicians as collaborators and advisors will need to be promoted with medical students and residents exposed early in their training. New technology such as remote involvement of team members for meetings, telehealth, and primary care patient portals to the electronic medical record, are novel ways to provide team-based care.

But the returns for establishing a team based primary care model in teaching institutions could be enormous. Such practices may be eligible for CMS model demonstrate grants and new reimbursement strategies tied to outcomes and partici-

Table 6.1 ACGME core competencies

Patient Care- experience in providing a team model of continuity of care, counseling and preventive services for patients and families
Medical knowledge- focusing on evidence-based primary care, prevention, screening, health promotion, chronic disease management, and health outcomes
Practice based learning and improvement- participation in practice based chronic disease management, setting and achieving quality care indicators, analyzing performance data
Systems Based Practice- supporting patients and families through transitions from hospital and nursing home back to home, facilitating home health care and other community based services, development of medical neighborhoods with specialty physicians supporting chronic disease management models, participation in accountable care organizations
Professionalism- developing collaborative models of care with other healthcare professionals particularly nurse practitioners and physician assistants, learning new physician management and consultative roles and relationships to support delivery models focused on improved health outcomes
Interpersonal Skills and Communication- with nurses, care managers, specialty physicians, patients and families

pation under alternative payment models (APM's). Revitalized team based primary care could help reverse the trend toward specialization among medical graduates [9], and increase the appeal of primary care practice to new generations of physicians adding to enhanced access and quality of care for patients. A team based outpatient primary care teaching model will help align medical education with predictable changes in the US healthcare delivery system [10].

GME will be held accountable for outcomes demanded by the public. The training of new geriatricians and primary care physicians requires that we connect with rising students and house staff as a represent the pipeline to future practice. New faculty especially, closer in age and training to students and housestaff, can help provide role models and develop and further nascent interests in Geriatrics and Primary Care.

References

1. Kocher R, Emanuel EJ, NM DP. The affordable care act and the future of clinical medicine: the opportunities and challenges. Ann Int Med. 2010;153:536–9.
2. White S, Powers JS. Effectiveness of an inpatient Geriatric Service in a University Hospital. J TN Med Assoc. 1994;87:425–8.
3. Powers JS, White S, Varnell L, et al. And autonomy supportive model of geriatric team function. Tennessee Medicine. 2000; pp. 295–7.
4. Deci EL, Ryan RM. Intrinsic motivation and self-determination in human behavior. New York: Plenum; 1985.
5. Deci EL, Eghvari H, Patrick BC, et al. Facilitating internalization: the self-determination. perspective. J Pers. 1994;62:119–42.
6. Ryan RM. Control and information in the interpersonal sphere, an extension of cognitive evaluation theory. J Pers Soc Psychol. 1982;43:56–461.450.

7. https://www.acgme.org/Portals/0/PDFs/ACGMEMilestones-CCC-AssesmentWebinar.pdf. Accessed 9 Apr 2017.
8. Paul S. Developing practice protocols for advanced practice nursing. AACN Clin Issue. 1999;10:343–55.
9. Brotherton SE, Etzel SI. Graduate medical education 2009–2010. JAMA. 2010;304:1255–70.
10. Models of care: Commonwealth funding, issue brief October 2015, publication 1843, vol 31.

Chapter 7
Selling to Management – Outpatient Care and Community Programs

Abstract The patient centered medical home model is being implemented by a growing number of health organizations in order to provide more comprehensive, coordinated, and patient centered care. This model may be a value-added means to manage frail elderly, contributing to cost avoidance and improved outcomes. The patient-centered healthcare model may be of value to health systems seeking to better manage the care complex older adults. This value-based model can be further augmented by the use of new technology to facilitate interactions with patients, family caregivers, and participating team members who may not all be present at the same location, in order to effectively function as a team.

In the US there is a great demand for Primary Care and outpatient services, but a declining number of medical trainees enter primary care each year. There are many reasons for this mismatch between the need for care and service availability including the high cost of medical education and large debts incurred by physicians in training, the generally poor reimbursement for Primary Care and its long hours, excessive administrative tasks, and the low prestige given to primary care by hospitals, health systems, and specialty colleagues. The situation is similar for Geriatrics. Consequently, there is a long patient waiting list for Primary Care and Geriatrics. This has helped stimulate the growth of advanced practice nurses and physician assistants who can care for an estimated 80% of primary care conditions and function well in a team based care model. A team-based primary care model can provide a patient centered medical home for Primary Careas well as Geriatrics, utilizing physician leadership of the healthcare team. This value-based model can be further augmented by the use of new technology to facilitate interactions with patients, family caregivers, and participating team members who may not all be present at the same location, in order to effectively function as a team.

A primary care outpatient geriatrics practice is difficult to sustain in isolation. Many physicians see geriatric patients included in their mix of younger patients in a general medicine or family practice setting. An exclusively geriatric practice presents many challenges to the physician including the level of complexity and the need for ancillary support from social work, nursing, and pharmacy. Large healthcare systems have employed geriatricians to focus on the management of complex older adults, and may have disease management programs targeted for certain

© Springer International Publishing AG 2017   37
J.S. Powers, *Creating a Value Proposition for Geriatric Care*, SpringerBriefs in
Health Care Management and Economics, DOI 10.1007/978-3-319-62271-2_7

conditions such as hypertension, diabetes, and congestive heart failure which provide telephone monitoring for selected patient populations.

The patient centered medical home (PCMH) model is being implemented by a growing number of health organizations in order to provide more comprehensive, coordinated, and patient- centered care. This new model of primary care is a re-design with a focus on population management, and alternative encounters such as group and telemedicine encounters [1]. The PCMH model includes team-based care focused on enhanced access and coordination. Published evaluations of PCMH are often limited to single practice or small groups of practices focusing on limited clinical conditions, and showing small positive effects on the patient experience, and measures of health care delivery. In 2010 the Veterans Health Administration (VHA) implemented the PCMH model (Patient- Aligned Care Teams – PACT) at all primary care clinics [2], presently including a population of five million veterans. A 3 year implementation experience showed PACT required a 3.0 FTEE staff per 1.0 FTEE provider ratio, but produced a 20% reduction in return visits and a tenfold increase in telephone care, making room for many new patient visits [3].

We adapted the PACT model to a geriatric practice in 2011. Over 50% of veterans receiving primary care are over age 65, with those over age 85 representing the fastest growing subpopulation which includes the most cognitively and physically disabled categories of patients. Geri-PACT is a special population of complex geriatric and other high risk vulnerable veterans requiring integrated, interdisciplinary assessment and longitudinal management and coordination of both VA and non-VA services for patients and caregivers, in order to achieve optimal results.

The Geri-PACT Team consists of the Geri-PACT provider (geriatrician or geriatric nurse practitioner serving a population of approximately 800), a social worker, a clinical pharmacist, a licensed vocational nurse, and clerical staff. These individuals function at the top of their licenses as experienced health professionals working as a coordinated unit delivering patient-centered assessments and managing medically complex and vulnerable elderly individuals. Patients and caregivers received frequent communications from the Geri-PACT Team including contact when hospitalized, and following discharge from hospital and long-term care facilities.

Example 7.1 A Grateful Patient (Sequel to Example 5.2, p. 28) Mr. G, a crusty 89-year-old veteran, is accustomed to driving 110 miles to come to the medical center for his primary care, urology, and cardiology visits. When told that his long-time primary care physician was retiring in that he was being referred to Geri-PACT he was dismayed and considered obtaining primary care at another location. However, soon after his primary care physician retired he presented to the Geri-PACT clinic without an appointment but experiencing crushing chest pain which he endured during his long drive to clinic, bypassing several emergency rooms. He was immediately checked in and evaluated by the Geri-PACT physician, and the EKG revealed his suspected crescendo angina. The Geri-PACT physician walked the EKG to the cardiologist and arranged immediate admission to the hospital where a cardiac catheterization revealed a left main coronary occlusion. Following coronary bypass surgery and a short skilled nursing home stay, the Geri-PACT Team followed his progress, arrange home care services and frequent follow-up in the Geri-PACT clinic as well as other specialty clinics. While still crusty and not afraid to express his expectations of all who serve him, Mr. G. continues to be a loyal Geri-PACT patient, grateful for the care he receives.

Planning for Geri-PACT began in 2010 with meetings of potential stakeholders and supporters with frequent PDSA improvement cycles oriented toward strategy, resource development, and clinical care process improvement. Geri-PACT developed from a part time geriatric evaluation and management clinic population which had been operating for 20 years. Staffing and space were obtained through cooperative arrangements and shared space with similarly small Neurology and Psychiatry outpatient clinics. An initial start-up grant from the Veterans Administration for new Transformational Models of Care for the twenty-first century was obtained to cover 0.5 FTEE Social Worker, Pharm.D., RN, and Advanced Practice Nurse was essential in obtaining leadership approval to initiate Geri-PACT. These personnel continued with other collateral duties in addition to Geri-PACT.

Our Geri-PACT proved to be a sick population, as expected [4]. The mean age was 84 years with 25% patients having diabetes, 15% dementia and 10% congestive heart failure in addition to multiple other medical comorbidities and an average 7% yearly mortality. Over a 4 year time frame, The Geri-PACT Team witnessed yearly hospitalizations reduced from 21–13%, mean number of medications per patient fell from 11–9, and the 30 day Hospital readmission rate fell from 35 to 6% for this population.

The successful implementation and early gains of Geri-PACT provided a helpful example in the early development of primary care PACT at our facility. In addition to sustaining the Geri-PACT program at our facility, regional leadership also became aware of Geri-PACT outcomes and its potential for implementation at other medical centers in the region. We were invited to present our model and early successes at meetings where cost avoidance was becoming a priority as administrators began to respond to new performance objectives related to value-based purchasing. As a result, leadership required Geri-PACT development as part of the 2015 strategic plan at all regional facilities. The following year regional leadership further provided first-year funding of approximately $3.5 million for six sites to locally develop and fully implement the Geri-PACT model throughout the region. The model is now also being actively promoted nationally within the VA system.

The Geri-PACT model may be a value-added means to manage frail elderly, contributing to cost avoidance and improved outcomes. Detailed evaluation of long-term outcomes and downstream effects on health care utilization patterns remains an ongoing endeavor. Key evaluation measures include organizational context, staffing components, team function and provider satisfaction, patient and caregiver needs and satisfaction, tracking of care transitions, and other performance and health outcomes metrics. We eagerly await aggregate outcome data from larger implementation programs.

The Geri-PACT program demonstrated the first patient centered medical home to the rest of the facility and served as a local model for all primary care services. The program was able to assimilate new requests for additional high–risk patient populations, including falls and dementia patient consultations, distant caregiver support through a telehealth portal, and palliative care patients with advanced disease processes.

The addition of other digital technology and social media to support busy caregivers could include telehealth for outreach to patients and caregivers at a distance, primary care patient portals to the electronic record to communicate with team members, group clinics for caregiver support and patient education, and virtual inclusion of additional extended team member consultants. The patient centered healthcare model may be of value to other health systems seeking to better manage the care of complex older adults. Health professions students also have found Geri-PACT to be an ideal site to learn inter-professional skills including team-based care.

References

1. Bodenheimer, Thomas, Grumbach, Kevin (UCSF Primary Care). Improving primary care: strategies and tools for a better practice. New York: McGraw-Hill; 2007. ISBN paperback 9780071447386.
2. Department of Veterans Affairs, Veterans Health Administration. Patient aligned care team (PACT) handbook. Washington, DC; 2014. https://www.va.gov/VHAPUBLICATIONS/ViewPublication.asp?pub_ID=2977. Accessed 23 Mar 2017.
3. Rosland AM, Nelson K, Sun H, Dolan ED, Maynard C, Bryson C, Stark R, Shear JM, Kerr E, Fihn SD, Schectman G. The patient-centered medical home in the Veterans Health Administration. Am J Manag Care. 2013; 19(7):e-263–272, 2–13.
4. Department of Veterans Affairs, Veterans Health Administration. Patient Aligned care team (Geri-PACT) handbook. Washington, DC; 2015. https://www.Va.Gov/vhapublications/ViewPublication.Asp?pub_ID=3115. Accessed 23 Mar 2017.

Chapter 8
Selling to Management – Inpatient Care

Abstract Older adults are at high risk for prolonged hospital stays, complications during the hospitalization, and early readmission. All health systems are under pressure to utilize hospital resources as efficiently as possible. Geriatric consultation and geriatrics units may be part of the future fabric of more hospitals caring for patients with delayed discharges and complex care needs. Improvement of functional status, begun early during the hospital stay and supported throughout the hospitalization, can improve outcomes without jeopardizing overall hospital length of stay or increased cost.

All health systems are under pressure to utilize hospital resources as efficiently as possible. Hospital beds represent the most expensive real estate anywhere, with daily rates upwards of $2500 daily [1]. University hospitals are also under pressure from accrediting bodies to decrease the size of services cared for by trainees. Inpatient mid-level providers are prevalent, and are natural allies for an inter-disciplinary senior-friendly service. Acute Care for Elderly (ACE) [2] services also help teach geriatrics to trainees of all health disciplines and they may improve the quality of care by more appropriately addressing care needs of older adults. This is especially helpful for patients at high risk for functional decline in order to achieve improved outcome measures such as discharge to lower levels of care and preventing early repeat hospitalizations. Improvement of functional status, begun early during the hospital stay and supported throughout the hospitalization, can indeed improve outcomes without jeopardizing overall hospital length of stay or increased cost [2].

Despite the best evidence-based rationale, however, a model program can sometimes be launched too early to be appreciated and adopted by administration. New leadership may not be able to embrace a new paradigm due to lack of training, perspective, and a lack of incentives to focus on its value. Appropriate buy-in of all stakeholders is important as the following example illustrates.

Example 8.1 A New Model of Care Ahead of Its Time An Acute Care for the Elderly ACE unit was initiated at the University Hospital, modeled after early descriptions of programs at UCLA and supported by the VA [3]. The interdisciplinary geriatric team consisted of a medical director/geriatrician, a gerontological advanced practice nurse, social worker, dietitian, pharmacist, and occupational and

J.S. Powers, *Creating a Value Proposition for Geriatric Care*, SpringerBriefs in Health Care Management and Economics, DOI 10.1007/978-3-319-62271-2_8

physical therapists. All team members were based in their respective departments with collateral duties, but functioned collaboratively in the care of the ACE service patients. The service was nurse-managed, had a an initial census of six and demonstrated a philosophy of care encompassing a shift in focus from acute illness- driven care to restorative, functional, and patient-centered care. Patients were derived from the geriatrician's outpatient practice as well as from consultations and hospital transfers from medical and surgical services, based on medical and functional status criteria. In general medically stable patients at risk for functional decline with rehabilitation potential were accepted on the service. At the time there were no other nurse practitioners practicing at the University Hospital. Despite support of the Nursing Service and other disciplines, in a matter of months, Internal Medicine Department administrators vehemently opposed the project and created numerous barriers to geriatric program development. This included opposing nurse practitioner billing provider status, cohorting of beds into a single unit to facilitate nursing staff communication, mandating detailed attending physician attestation to team notes, and prohibiting resident coverage and rotation on the service. The ACE Unit persisted however, and slowly grew as a natural experiment over a 20 year period, spanning and surviving several different administrations. The ACE unit now has over 20 patients with 3 nurse practitioners and serves as the base for the Internal Medicine's inpatient teaching geriatric service. Many other hospital services have emulated the geriatrics program and there are now over 200 nurse practitioners practicing at the University Hospital include intensive care units, surgical services, and many other inpatient and outpatient specialty programs.

The VA has also recognized the need to improve efficiency of inpatient care (SAIL Metrics, Chap. 5). The case is particularly important for high-risk elderly and dementia patients. At our facility at any time there were approximately 20 high-risk patients remaining in acute care beds with rehabilitation and disposition concerns and exhibiting excessive length of stay. The Veterans Administration permits a designation of Intermediate Care as a separate category of patients between acute care and long-term care, with a maximum average length of stay of 30 days. Intermediate Care is a level of care appropriate for patients who no longer require acute medical care and face a prolonged stay in the hospital. A task force on dementia care confirmed that many medically complex patients have dementia complicating their care and that 80% were appropriate for Intermediate Care. We developed a Geriatric Evaluation and Management (GEM) [4] interdisciplinary team to provide a comprehensive evaluation and treatment plan for these patients. The team consisted of a medical director/geriatrician, advanced practice nurse, and a social worker. Extended team members included a dedicated pharmacist, physical and occupational therapists all based in their respective departments but functioning collaboratively and with collateral duties.

Example 8.2 A Model Program Catches On (Sequel to Example 6.1, p.32) The Geriatric Evaluation and Management Service inter-professional inpatient service cares for complex elderly and dementia patients at high risk for re-admission. Over a 20 year history it has ranged in size from 6–10 beds and has positively impacted the acute care service at length of stay. Patients are seen on a consult basis and transferred to GEM with a focus on rehabilitation, discharge to a lower level of care, assistance with transitions of care, and difficult dispositions. Recent quality metrics from operations data indicated that GEM demonstrated a 30% medication reduction (average number of medicines reduced from 15 to 10), 25% Nursing Home placement reduction compared to the original discharge plan, and a 10% 30 day acute care readmission rate, approximately half of the facility's 30 day return rate. With the introduction of new SAIL performance metrics, the administration has now expressed interest in increasing the size of the bed service, with appropriate additional resources, in order to accommodate increased numbers of dementia and complex care patients on the acute services, with data estimates of a $3 million yearly cost avoidance compared to usual care. (Sequel … Example 10.1, p. 53)

Geriatrics units may be part of the future fabric of more hospitals, caring for patients with delayed discharge and complex care needs. Geriatric hospitalists may serve as consultants for specialty colleagues to reduce transitions of care failures, to improve communication between levels of care, and to facilitate the provision of community resources in order to guarantee a successful return to the home and community. Consider the prospects of utilizing video conferencing to enlarge the virtual discharge planning team to include hospitalists, home health and nursing home personnel, the primary care provider and geriatric consultants for selected high risk patients to facilitate the management of geriatric syndromes and polypharmacy, recommend appropriate community resources, and provide better communication and to allow return to the primary care provider in a timely manner to prevent repeat hospitalizations.

References

1. The Agency for Healthcare Research and Quality (AHRQ). 2014 estimates average cost hospital stay (4.5 days) $10,885, with per-diem $2,366. http://www.ahrq.gov/research/findings/factsheets/index.html. Accessed 13 Feb 2017.
2. Fox MT, Sidani S, Persaud M, Tregunno D, Maimets I, Brooks D, O'Brien K. Acute care for elders components of acute geriatric unit care: systematic descriptive review. J Am Geriatr Soc. 2013;61:939–46.
3. White S, Powers JS. Effectiveness of an inpatient geriatric service in a University Hospital. J TN Med Assoc. 1994;87:425–8.
4. Hauser B, Laubacher M, Robinson J, Powers JS. Evaluation of an intermediate care and geriatric unit in a VA Hospital. South Med J. 1991;84:597–602.

Chapter 9
Selling to Management – Transitions of Care, Home Health and Nursing Home Care

Abstract Because the hospital is the major component of a healthcare system and provides the most expensive services, it is natural to focus on acute care. However neglecting other elements of care across the patient care continuum puts performance objectives at risk, harms the patient experience of care, and increases cost. Value-based purchasing has forced administrators to consider cost avoidance as an important and critical part of the business plan. CMS is clear that performance objectives for hospitals include adhering to performance objectives. These mandates constitute very important levers. It remains to be seen how healthcare systems will responded to new inpatient and outpatient quality reporting metrics with heavy financial penalties for noncompliance.

Value–based purchasing is a demand side strategy to reward quality and health care delivery. Effective healthcare services and high-performing healthcare providers are incentivized to provide quality outcomes and to control costs. Value base purchasing requires healthcare systems to strategize by considering all elements of the continuum of patient care. Covered beneficiaries enrolled in the healthcare system must be efficiently managed at each level of care. Appropriate acknowledgment, communication, and respect for each component of healthcare along the continuum is essential for optimum patient experience of care, outcome performance, and cost avoidance [1–4]. Because the hospital is the major component of a healthcare system and provides the most expensive services, it is natural to focus on acute care. However neglecting other elements of care across the continuum puts the entire healthcare system performance objectives at risk, jeopardizes the patient experience of care, and increases cost. Value-based purchasing has forced administrators to consider cost avoidance as an important and critical part of the business plan. Now cost avoidance is the new cost center, essential to minimizing downside (loss) risk.

But culture change can be slow. How does a leader promote change despite a reluctant administration? Perhaps your healthcare system has behaved similarly.

Example 9.1 Continuing to Tilt Windmills The Geriatric Service has constantly pointed out opportunities for improvement to administration. Always a leader in specialty care and a preferred provider for referral services in the community, the

© Springer International Publishing AG 2017   45
J.S. Powers, *Creating a Value Proposition for Geriatric Care*, SpringerBriefs in
Health Care Management and Economics, DOI 10.1007/978-3-319-62271-2_9

university hospital was determined to maintain its advantage in the marketplace under fee-for-service. For many years the University Hospital built its reputation providing excellent specialty care and training, but to the neglect of Primary Care and Geriatrics. A home health service was started by the University as a lost leader, often operating in the red (financially separate accounting), to more quickly accept patients with complex care needs discharged from the hospital. The administration continued on an aggressive course to build more ICU beds and a hospitalist-based acute care program. It acknowledged the importance of Primary Care but preferred to build networks of referring hospitals and health systems who would maintain their own primary care capacity. The geriatrics program advised and supported the home health program, encouraging the adoption of specialty programs including wound care, mental health, infusion services, pharmacist-based medication reconciliation and advanced practice nurse p.r.n. house calls to serve the complex patient population. A telehealth program for disease management of diabetes, hypertension, and congestive heart failure produced early good results for several different quality indicators. However, extension of care management to network practices remained unsuccessful. A small program to affiliate with two nursing homes staffed by university physicians and advanced practice nurses remains ongoing but with little desire on the part of the administration to expand into a long term care network. The health system continues to respond slowly to new CMS quality indicator reporting requirements and alternative payment models, hoping that a new electronic medical record system with dashboards will facilitate the quality reporting process. Administration continues to direct its cost avoidance focus on a small cohort of special needs patients with high utilization rates, and enhanced discharge planning among hospital-based physicians. Geriatrics program models such as the patient centered medical home are considered interesting, but have not been embraced. Indeed, due to increasing growth of local population, a new certificate of need is being sought to increase bed capacity at the main hospital, with plans to displace existing primary care clinics located at the main medical center. So…round 2 begins! Perhaps this is an opportunity to create an outpatient center, to redesign and reinvigorate primary care and advance new models of care? Be sure to keep a place at the table – as with change comes opportunity.

CMS is clear that performance objectives for hospitals include adhering to performance objectives. These mandates constitute very important levers. It is unclear how many healthcare systems will responded to meet new inpatient and outpatient quality reporting metrics with heavy financial penalties for noncompliance. They also risk of loss of market share as competing institutions develop network affiliations with community referral resources. Healthcare systems are financially encouraged by CMS with higher reimbursement to participate in alternative payment models (APM's) such as Accountable Care Organizations (may have upside and downside risk), medical homes, disease bundling programs, and Medicare Shared Savings Programs (MSSP) which carry no downside risk. Outpatient APM's include focused disease-management programs, and physician payment models tied to quality targets.

The Veterans Health Administration (VA) is also transforming the culture of care in nursing homes, and enhancing care transitions and communication among care programs as part of its quality improvement program. The VA is responsible for managing nursing home patients at three levels of long term care (LTC): Community Living Centers (CLC), State Veterans Homes (SVH), and contracted Community Nursing Homes (CNH). CLC's are facilities run and staffed by the VA, SVH's are constructed with joint VA-state support but are managed privately, and CNH's which are privately owned and operated, provide care to Veterans in the community. The VA surveys care to provide oversight and to optimize resident care in long term care (LTC) facilities and spent $767 million in FY 2013 for contracted community nursing home care [5].

Example 9.2 Enhancing Accountability Regional executive leadership recognized that the long-term care survey process could be enhanced by standardizing the CNH survey process by reinforcing the accuracy and consistency of surveys so that it would be objective and consistent among facilities and that the VA would be a better informed purchaser of care. The geriatric service assisted with an implementation process to enhance the consistency of organizational oversight. This process included planning, engaging local buy-in and support, developing evaluation teams, marketing the need for a standardized inspection process, and stimulating an evaluation process for best practices compliance. The strategy for change implementation conformed to the Four Stage Model for organizational stages of change (Modern Organizational Theory – Table 4.4) [6] and the PARIHS implementation framework (Table 4.3) [7] including (1) Awareness of the variability of survey practices and cultural differences at the different facilities, (2) Identification of key personnel as content experts and agents of change, educating survey teams regarding evidence-based advances in LTC quality assurance, and change process recommendations based on best practices, (3) Implementation involving all stakeholders, expert opinion, and careful planning, engaging support for resources over a 2 year period, reflecting on strategy utilizing a modified Delphi process with frequent committee teleconferences, and (4) Institutionalization achieved by creation of a committee reporting structure comprised of the participants and aligned with the Regional Geriatric Service Line, data entry to the VA National NH Certification data base, and by planned regular review of LTC quality indicators with monthly committee conference calls to contribute to standardization, peer mentorship, and continued process improvement [8]. Because the VA has long been responsible for costs and outcomes across the continuum of care, leadership further requested Geriatric program involvement to help improve communication between the Home-Based Primary Care program (HBPC), Veterans Community Partnerships with Area Agencies on Aging/Disability (AAA/D), and VA regional community-based outpatient clinics (CBOC's) utilizing telehealth technologies for consultations to improve dementia care, caregiver support, and geriatric care of complex older patients residing at a distance from the medical center.

The work ahead is clear. There remains a major effort to encourage health systems see the benefits of supporting care across the continuum, to share resources to enhance care components across the continuum and to improve communication across the continuum. Development of patient-centered medical homes, disease management programs, and creating a real partnership and shared resources with other contributing components of healthcare networks are critical in order to support smooth transitions of care, minimize cost, and optimize patient outcome objectives for healthcare systems.

References

1. Naylor MD, Brooten DA, Campbell RL, Maislin G, McCauley KM, Schwartz JS. Transitional care of older adults hospitalized with heart failure: a randomized, controlled trial. J Am Geriatr Soc. 2004;52:675–84.
2. Ouslander J, Lamb G, Tappan R, et al. Interventions to reduce hospitalizations from nursing homes: evaluation of the INTERACT II collaborative quality improvement project. J Am Geriatr Soc. 2011;59:745–53.
3. Coleman EA, Smith JD, Frank JC, Min S, Parry C, Kramer AM. Preparing patients and caregivers to participate in care delivered across settings: the care transitions intervention. J Am Geriatr Soc. 2004;42:1817–25.
4. Vasilevskis EE, Ouslander JG, Mixon AS, Bell SP, Jacobsen JM, Saraf AA, Markley D, Sponsler KC, Shutes J, Long EA, Kripalani S, Simmons SF, Schnelle JF. Potentially avoidable readmissions of patients discharged to post-acute care: perspectives of hospital in skilled nursing facility staff. J Am Ger Soc. 2017;65:269–76.
5. Veterans Health Administration. OIG, Office of Audits and Evaluations: Audit of the Community Nursing Home Program, No. 11-0031-160; 29 March 2013
6. Steckler A, Goodman R, Kegler MC. Mobilizing organizations for health enhancement: theories of organizational change. In: Glanz K, Rimer BK, Lewis FM, editors. Health behavior and health education: theory, research and practice. 3rd ed. San Francisco: Jossey-Bass; 2002. pp. 335–60.
7. Rycroft-Malone J. The PARIHS framework–a framework for guiding the implementation of evidence–based practice. J Nurs Care Qual. 2004;19:297–304.
8. Powers JS, Preshong M, Smith P. A model of regulatory alignment to enhance the long term care survey process in a Veterans healthcare network. Am J Med Qual. 2016;31:470–5.

Chapter 10
Epilogue

Abstract This final chapter is a checklist. It is also a summary of the major points covered in previous chapters, and addresses the topic of succession. The primary directive of the change agent is that the main purpose of the program is to benefit the institution. Well-intentioned healthcare professionals are often knowledgeable, idealistic, and logical. However, no justification for a program is sufficient to convince others, motivate an implementation team, or to create change. The change agent must sustain a passionate vision as well as a strategy for change. Change takes time, and the agent of change do not control the time line. He must be cognizant of the many steps involved in achieving and sustaining organizational change. Many reforms are incremental without immediately obvious results.

This chapter is a checklist.

So, you have an idea, a new model that we will address an identified gap in care ✓
You have a well-conceived vision about the future will look like with improvements to care ✓
You have a focused and well-defined mission ✓
You have a compelling argument ✓
But it's not enough!

Medical people are easy to spot – knowledgeable, idealistic, and logical. These are all wonderful traits. Perhaps a desire to serve and make changes for the better is what drew you to the medical field. Medical people are also trained in empathy skills and the ability to see things from others' perspective. This talent is an extremely valuable negotiating skill. However, no justification for a program is sufficient to convince others, motivate an implementation team, or obtain resources to create change. You also need a strategy. And remember, the primary directive of the change agent is that the main purpose of the program is to benefit the institution.

Change takes time. You will be successful if you build coalitions, but you cannot control the time line of change. Change may not be linear and many enabling factors and pre-work will be required. This is demonstrated by Kotter's eight steps for organizational change. Complex interventions require a systems approach. Many reforms are incremental without immediately obvious results.

J.S. Powers, *Creating a Value Proposition for Geriatric Care*, SpringerBriefs in Health Care Management and Economics, DOI 10.1007/978-3-319-62271-2_10

Table 10.1 Developer-
change agents skills

1.	Future oriented
2.	Persistence
3.	Ability to market, rebrand
4.	Remain helpful
5.	Seek overlapping benefits
6.	Arrange new alliances, reformulate teams
7.	Be grateful

Table 10.2 Developer-
change agents tools

1.	Historical perspective
2.	Reflect from external framework
3.	Process orientation
4.	Be helpful

Change requires a champion who is knowledgeable about content but also has a mission and a talent for marshalling resources from many different sources. This champion also has to be resilient, willing to spend many volunteer hours towards attainment of the goal, and willing to sustain the program during times of decreased support and through funding cycles with gaps in resources.

Tables in this chapter are highlighted as resource tools for the agent of change to use as best fits the circumstances and program needs. These needs may change during the developmental cycle of the program, and the author has used all of these tools at different times.

The agent of change must possess a number of skills (Table 10.1). He must be future oriented and above all be persistent at efforts which may take years before recognizable accomplishments are apparent. The change agent must be able to market, constantly reframe and rebrand, and always remain helpful. The agent of change must cultivate coalitions by realizing the overlapping benefits to all contributors while maintaining a focus on the greater common good. The change agent is continually arranging new alliances and reformulating strategies. Additionally the champion must be always grateful to all contributors to the cause.

The agent of change has many tools to utilize (Table 10.2). These include a historical perspective so as not to repeat the same mistakes as others. The agent of change must also inspect the product from an external viewpoint, seeking and valuing perspectives given by many others which help guide strategy and program design to reflect the common good. The agent of change must possess and respect a process orientation. And the agent of change must also be helpful. This last tool creates many alliances, contributions, and collaborations to help develop as well as sustain programs.

Incentives guide all human behavior. Positive incentives include recognition, influence, positive performance outcomes and financial benefits. Negative influences include fines/punishments, costs, regulations, and loss of public image.

Table 10.3 Selling to management

1.	Effective and compelling business case
2.	Interest based negotiation creates value for both sides
3.	Triple aim of IOM
	Improved care experience for the patient
	Improved quality of care
	Cost efficiency (including cost avoidance)

Table 10.4 Stages of organizational change

1.	Awareness
2.	Identification
3.	Implementation
4.	Institutionalization

Always consider creating proposals with overlapping goals and program objectives. A win-win approach first is always recommended.

Strategy – the change agent must not only have a passionate vision and a compelling program but a strategy for sustainment through the potentially long implementation timeline and to overcome numerous barriers and invested interests maintaining the status-quo.

Selling to management requires possession of an effective and compelling business case to create interest-based negotiations and value for both sides. (Table 10.3) In a value-based healthcare system, cost avoidance can be a valuable currency. The triple aims of the Institute of Medicine help provide an ethical grounding to program models by contributing to (1) An improved care experience for the patient, (2) Improved quality outcomes, and (3) Cost efficiency, including cost avoidance.

The change agent must be aware of the processes and stages of organizational change (Table 10.4) including (1) Awareness of a problem or gap in the current provision of care, (2) Identification of resources and strategies to address these gaps, (3) The change agent must realize that the implementation needs to be strategically timed in order to achieve early success and, (4) Work for sustainment to lead to final institutionalization and acceptance and sustainment.

The change agent would be wise to realize that there may be as many as eight steps to change. (Table 10.5) The agent of change must (1) First set the stage by creating a sense of urgency, (2) Pull together and guide the team, (3) Develop a change in vision and strategy based on organizational needs, (4) Communicate to others to obtain understanding and buy-in, (5) Empower others to act, to achieve ownership and to further support the program, (6) Promote short-term wins for continued support and sustainment, and to (7) Realize that change takes time, perhaps years and to not let up. (8) Finally the change agent must make the program stick by creating a new culture, organize support for sustainment producing continuing returns on the investment and increased value to all contributors.

Table 10.5 Kotter's
eight-step framework

1.	Create a sense of urgency
2.	Pull together the guiding team
3.	Develop the change in vision and strategy
4.	Communicate for understanding and buy-in
5.	Empower others to act
6.	Promote short-term wins
7.	Don't let up
8.	Create a new culture

Table 10.6 PDSA
improvement cycle

1.	Plan
2.	Do
3.	Study (check)
4.	Act

Table 10.7 SMART
processes

Specific
Measurable
Attainable
Relevant
Time- bound

PDSA improvement cycles can be a great way to understand and adjust strategies. (Table 10.6) (1) So you've planned a compelling program ✓, (2) So you've strategically implemented a program to achieve early success ✓, (3) But you have identified barriers must reformulate your strategy✓, (4) You then redirect your activities ✓. Each step of the change process (Table 10.7) should be specific, measurable, obtainable, relevant, and time bound. Welcome to the world of the change agent!

This book would be incomplete without some discussion of succession planning, techniques to make programs transition–worthy [1] and foster the training of others to carry on the work begun by the agent of change. Permanent direction of a new program by the change agent is not sustainable. The change agent must ensure that programs and services continue to operate and are sustained beyond the tenure of the inaugural leader. Our experience has been that creating the program for the benefit of the institution rather than for any specific individual is critical. Program ownership must be collective. A wise leader realizes that succession planning is a necessary component of program development. Graceful relinquishing of control and direction of the program is critical to successful transitions and program sustainment.

Example 10.1 Succession Planning – If the future Doesn't Exist, Create It! (Sequel to Examples 6.1, p. 32 and 8.2, p. 42) The geriatric unit was finally recognized for its positive influence on the hospital's quality metrics. New leadership had secured the resources to sustain the program with every expectation that it would grow in importance and scope of activity. The agent of change realized that the mentoring, coaching and advocacy that had been so critical to nurturing the program early on now needed to give way to exiting. Importantly, the program had grown and required much more time and effort than could be safely done with part-time availability. A full-time medical director position was created and staff educated on the growth and mission of the program and prepared for changes over a several month time frame. A new director would be new to them and the team would need time to adapt. An experienced medical director was selected. After arriving the change agent shared call with the new director to ease the transition, and continued to meet with the team at regular weekly patient care conferences to facilitate the transition. The new director was closely engaged in meeting facility leadership and understanding the history and mission of the program. Additionally they were placed on relevant facility quality improvement committees and became familiar with institutional needs and resources and oriented to all aspects of the position. The new director expressed complementary but somewhat different views regarding patient admission criteria, scheduling, documentation, and communication preferences. These were accepted and the team adjusted over a 6-month period.

There is unlikely to be already supply of individuals ready to replace change agents and to assume the direction of a program, particularly one involving new care models. The inaugural leader must train new leaders during the course of program execution giving clear messages regarding the vision and performance objectives. Not all potential leadership candidates will accept the responsibilities offered. New program leaders must necessarily be self-motivated in order to be fulfilled as well as successful. Personal or family issues or a desire to create one's own program can be important considerations for potential candidates. In the fields of Geriatrics and Palliative Care where the number of opportunities exceeds the number of qualified candidates, excellent opportunities abound and successful trainees who ultimately take positions elsewhere will always reflect positively on their mentors.

A successful transition (Table 10.8) requires preparation of the team, good communication, and a gradual reduction in the influence of the inaugural leader. Team

Table 10.8 Succession planning key points	Permanent leadership is not sustainable, create the future
	Maintaining program vision and objectives by preparing all for leadership transitions
	Train new leadership and give the freedom to experiment
	Permit and facilitate expressions of reaction to change
	Focus on the program mission and future vision

members may experience difficulty with change and respond with anger and abandonment. This is understandable as the new team must progress through Tuckman's developmental sequence of group function: (1) Forming, (2) Storming, (3) Norming, and (4) Performing [2]. However the wise leader must challenge all team members to be professional and to focus on achieving excellent clinical outcomes and upholding the usefulness of the program to the institution, supporting service needs. It is important for the exiting leader to continue support during the transition, focusing on group needs and specific requests of the team. The change agent must support the new leader, and let all team members know that they also remain valuable contributors.

The change agent's message must be clearly articulated: We (Geriatricians) have skills to improve the patient experience of care with quality metrics to support our claims. Let us help add value to our health care system by embracing value-based healthcare transformation. The future may be hard to see however the agent of change can contribute to and create that future. Despite many potential barriers, culture change is eventually guaranteed, the public demanding it.

A Final Encouragement
May The Road Rise Up To Meet You [3]
May the road rise up to meet you.
May the wind be always at your back.
May the sun shine warm upon your face;
the rains fall soft upon your fields
and until we meet again,
May God hold you in the palm of His hand.

References

1. Executive Transitions. www.compasspoint.org. Accessed 25 Mar 2017.
2. Tuckman BW. Developmental sequence in small groups. Psych Bull. 1965;63:384–99.
3. Traditional Gaelic Blessing.

Printed in the United States
By Bookmasters